THE

SCHOOL
MANAGEMENT
HANDBOOK

1994

Edited by

Howard Green

**KOGAN
PAGE**

First edition published in 1992

This (third) edition published in 1994

Kogan Page Ltd
120 Pentonville Road
London N1 9JN

British Library Cataloguing in Publication Data
A CIP record for this book is available from the British Library.
ISBN 0 7494 1224 0
ISSN 1351–4660

Printed and bound in England by Clays Ltd, St Ives plc

RISO DIGITAL PRINTING
TECHNOLOGY

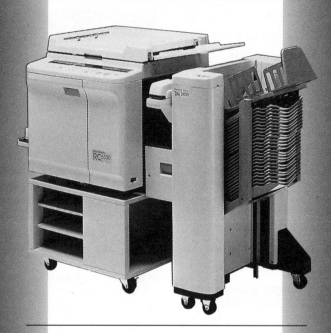

ACHIEVES DRAMATIC
COST SAVINGS ON PRINTING
AND COPYING BILLS

WHICH IS WHY INPLANT LITHO & PHOTOCOPY DUPLICATING SYSTEMS WILL CONTINUE TO BE REPLACED BY THE RISO DIGITAL PRINTING METHOD

RISO UK LTD
4 COMMERCIAL WAY, ABBEY ROAD INDUSTRIAL PARK
PARK ROYAL, LONDON, NW10 7EX
TELEPHONE: 081 838 0404 FAX: 081 961 7200

RISO PRODUCTS ARE DISTRIBUTED THROUGH AUTHORISED DEALERS ONLY

Contents

5

PART THREE: FINANCIAL MANAGEMENT

PART FOUR: HUMAN RESOURCE MANAGEMENT

Contents

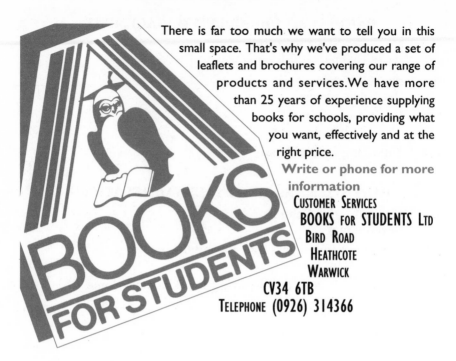

Foreword

To manage a school is an awesome enough task these days. It is as though the government has decided to distract school management by regularly lobbing hand grenades of externally-imposed change into the daily business of schooling. And schools are places where there is no shortage of crisis.

As this volume shows, managing the school is only half the task. Schools need to be 'led': those inside them, principally teachers and pupils but also governors and parents, need to know that their leaders share a passion for learning. It is not too much to say that a school will start to decline when the leader becomes preoccupied either with the 'external' role and demands of leadership or with the 'systems' and 'functions' of the school's management. Of course both these activities are important; indeed to ignore them would be dangerous and foolhardy. Nevertheless, the interest of the leaders in teaching, and especially in learning, is the key to school success. This interest will express itself in language, in the use of time and in priorities. The community will know that their leaders are truly fascinated by the mysteries of learning and are themselves learning something new all the time.

That message – central to the task of the post-holder with responsibility, head of department, head of year, deputy or head – has never been put more at risk by the avalanche of change and the deconcentration of tasks which have been shifted from the LEA to the school and college.

This volume will help leaders and managers cope with that external change. They will see how the Development Plan can be a means of spinning out to a reasonable time-scale what is essentially an unreasonable management expectation. They will learn to juggle priorities, time and money.

Indeed, in different ways the contributors all shed light on the seven essential processes of school improvement – leadership, management, the environment, teaching and learning, collective review, staff development and parental involvement. It is sobering for me as someone who has been fascinated by the emerging research evidence on school effectiveness and school improvement, to see how our knowledge of these seven processes has grown exponentially.

Leaders at any level in the schools will, I think, need the four qualities which I heard an American once describe as the essentials of leadership – intellectual curiosity; regarding crisis as the norm and complexity as fun; an unquenchable sense of unwarranted optimism; and a complete absence of paranoia or self-pity.

Of course the real challenge is to make sure that knowledge is distilled and widely shared by the leaders in the nation's schools. This volume should help that process, and the prize will be each successive generation exceeding the educational achievements of its predecessors. No previous age has even attempted as much.

Tim Brighouse
Chief Education Officer
Birmingham City Council

Preface

The School Management Handbook aims to provide its readers with a series of short, informative articles about some of the key issues affecting the management of schools today. The target audience are all those concerned, directly or indirectly, with school management: heads, deputies, governors, those aspiring to such positions, those studying aspects of school management and those advising and training school managers.

The first two editions were well received and clearly met a need. In this third edition we have added several new articles on important topics like the 1993 Education Bill, Managing School Inspection and Special Needs. There has also been some restructuring of the Handbook to provide more cohesiveness, particularly with an early series of articles on Whole-School Management Planning.

We hope that previous readers will appreciate the changes in this third edition and that new readers will find the Handbook helpful and comprehensive. We are in the business of 'continuous improvement' and the publishers would welcome suggestions for alterations and additions for future editions.

Effective management is a means to an end: the development and enhancement of children's learning in our schools through the successful deployment, support and motivation of staff. We must avoid the trap of school management becoming an end in itself.

It is also important not to confuse 'management' with 'leadership'. The former is about achieving tasks by, with and through people; the latter should provide the values and vision that serve as a framework within which the tasks of management take place.

The authors are all experienced practitioners in the fields that they are writing about. Our thanks are due to them for finding the time to contribute in already overcrowded schedules.

Howard Green
Eggbuckland
Plymouth

The Contributors

Joan Atkins is a Health and Safety Officer with Devon Local Education Authority.

Hazel Barker is Senior Consultant at Calderdale College's training and consultancy company, Calderdale Associates Ltd.

Margaret Bell is Chief Executive of the National Council for Educational Technology (NCET).

Mike Bell is Headteacher of one of the first schools in England and Wales to achieve self-governing status.

Bill Berry is Headteacher of Bartholomew School in Oxford.

Ken Biggs is Headteacher of Chew Valley School, Chew Magna, Bristol.

Tim Brighouse is Chief Education Officer of Birmingham City Council Education Department.

John Chastney is a Partner in Neville Russell Chartered Accountants.

David Cook is Director of Education at Lincolnshire County Council.

Maureen Cruikshank is Principal of The Beauchamp College in Oadby, Leicestershire.

John Curtis-Rouse is Vice-Principal of Eggbuckland Community College, Plymouth.

John Davies is a consultant specialising in implementing and running accounting and related software computer systems.

The Contributors

Chris Doak is a Health and Safety Officer with Devon Local Education Authority.

Jim Donnelly is Headteacher of Litherland High School, Sefton, Merseyside and is author of several books on educational management published by Kogan Page.

Bruce Douglas is Principal of Branston Community College and Legal Secretary of the Secondary Heads Association.

Peter Downes is Headteacher of Hinchingbrooke School in Huntingdon.

John Dunford is the Headteacher of Durham Johnston Comprehensive School, Durham.

Peter Earley is Senior Research Officer in Professional Studies at the National Foundation for Educational Research.

Roger Fetherston is Vice-Principal of Eggbuckland Community College, Plymouth.

Laurence French is Coordinator of Marketing and Public Relations, Campion School, Leamington Spa.

Ron Glatter is Director of the Centre for Educational Policy and Management at the Open University.

Howard Green is Principal of Eggbuckland Community College, Plymouth, Devon. He was the first Director of the National Education Assessment Centre for Headteachers at Oxford and before that Head of the Henry Box School, Witney, Oxfordshire.

Barry Hilditch is Headteacher of Royston Comprehensive School, Barnsley.

Howard Jackson is the Financial Administration Manager at Bacup and Rawtenstall Grammar School in Lancashire.

Danny Lewis is Head of Learning Resources at Eggbuckland Community College in Plymouth.

Chris Lowe is Headteacher of Price William School in Northamptonshire.

Donald McIntyre is Reader in Educational Studies at Oxford University and an experienced researcher and theorist of teacher education. He is also co-author of *Mentoring* and *The School Mentor Handbook*, both published by Kogan Page.

Margaret Nicholls is Headteacher of Woodway Park Comprehensive School, Coventry.

David Nichols is Headteacher of Littleover Community School in Derby.

Dee Palmer-Jones is Headteacher of Brackenhoe School in Middlesbrough, Cleveland.

David Pardey is Managing Director of QIMM Development and is author of *Marketing for Schools*, published by Kogan Page.

Geoff Rhodes is Head of sixth form at Larkmead School in Abingdon, Oxfordshire.

Joan Sallis is a writer and lecturer on school governors and their development, and is a visiting professor at Nottingham University.

Brian Unwin is a Field Officer for the Secondary Heads Association and an educational consultant.

Andre Wagstaff is a Programme Manager at the National Council for Educational Technology (NCET).

Michael Warrington is Headteacher of the Radclyffe School in Oldham.

John West-Burnham is a lecturer in Educational Management at the University of Leicester.

Ben Whitney is specialist Education Welfare Officer at Staffordshire County Council. He is also author of *The Children Act and Schools*, published by Kogan Page.

Trevor Yates is Principal of Paignton Community College, Paignton, Devon.

Part One

The National Context for Managing Schools

1.1

The 1993 Education Reform Act in its Legislative Context

Bruce Douglas

The 1993 Education Reform Act, (the 'Act') described as a 'landmark Bill' by the Secretary of State during its passage into law, is the largest ever piece of educational legislation. Regarded by its proposers as the legal culmination of a revolution, leading through Local Management of Schools (LMS), to Grant-maintained Status (GMS) and to local and consumer power, it is seen by its opponents as an historic centralisation of power to ministers and ministerially appointed quangos, and as a blind act of a blind faith in market forces and competition to produce an adequate public service.

But whatever admiring or opposing view one takes, there is no denying that the Act makes many important legislative changes. Around 100,000 words in length, it is divided into six main sections (308 clauses and 21 schedules).

Section One

The first section re-writes the opening of the 1944 Act, and gives the Secretary of State the duty to 'promote education' by using his powers over 'bodies in receipt of public money'. (This new phase omits specific reference to Local Education Authorities (LEAs) and emphasises the new autonomy of LMS and GMS schools.) The Secretary of State must act with a view to 'improving standards, encouraging diversity and increasing opportunities for choice' –

17

words which could have many an interesting interpretation in the future, but in the current context obviously reflect the White Paper 'Choice & Diversity' and refer to the further establishment of grant-maintained schools, technology colleges, CTCs and other sponsored institutions of a distinctive style, and to parental choice in general.

But the main business of the first section of the Act is to establish the funding authorities. These new bodies are to take over from the Department for Education (DFE) the administration/funding of the growing GM sector (though it was insisted during parliamentary debate that they would be 'light touch' bodies).

Funding authorities assume the power to provide primary and secondary school places when the Secretary of State passes a Section 12(a) order (which he cannot do until ten per cent of the pupils of the relevant age-group in an LEA are in GM schools). However, the LEA retains the overall *duty* to provide sufficient school places, under Section 12(i)b (only possible when 75 per cent of the relevant pupils are in GM schools or if the Secretary of State agrees to an earlier LEA request). At this point all such functions pass to the funding authority.

Finally, Section One gives an important new power to the LEA to direct the admission of refused or excluded pupils to schools (including to GM schools) except to a school that has previously excluded the individual.

Section Two

Section Two of the Act, accounting for almost half of its total, re-enacts, with extensions, the 1988 Education Reform Act provisions relating to GM schools. Changes and additions are intended to promote GMS in general and the entry of business/industrial sponsorship of schools.

For example, governing bodies now need to pass only one resolution in order to initiate a ballot of parents in GMS, and by law must consider annually whether or not to do so. Time-scales, from resolution to ballot and positive ballot to GMS submission, are reduced (from 12 to 10 weeks and from six to four months).

The funding authority can propose a new GM school in an area where it operates, and (in a late change to the Bill) so can 'promoters' at any time, (whether there are existing GM schools in the LEA or not). 'Promoters' are to be asked to pay at least 15 per cent of the capital costs, but there are still likely to be many groups (for example with particular ethnic or religious affiliations) applying to set up their 'own' schools. Approval is meant to depend upon the extent of 'need', but in most cases there is both a 'market need' (ie parents willing to send children to such a school) *and* a 'market surplus' (ie the new school is likely to create an expensive surplus of under-capacity usage in neighbouring schools). The competing rhetorics of 'consumer choice' and 'efficiency' may between them pose the Secretary of State some difficult questions.

Section Two allows groups of GM schools to come together under a single governing body (of the usual size, except that each *head* teacher has the right to membership). Separate governing bodies may also form a joint committee and delegate joint business to it. In an attempt to invite marketing and business into the school system 'sponsors', in return for significant support (not specified), may nominate up to four 'sponsor governors'.

Section Three

Section Three, on Special Needs, only occupies around ten per cent of the Act, but effects important changes. Virtually the entire 1981 Act is repealed (though its main thrusts are re-written in post-ERA terms). LEAs are confirmed (not withstanding GMS) as the bodies responsible for the identification of and provision for Special Educational Needs (SEN). As such they will have the right of entry to, and monitoring of, SEN in all schools.

Parental choice is enshrined in SEN law. Parents' wishes about where a child with SEN is placed must normally be followed, though they can be overridden. The old threefold test remains: Does a placement (a) provide for the SEN identified; (b) not conflict with the provision to other pupils in the institution; (c) make efficient use of resources. There is a presumption that integration into mainstream schooling will be attempted if possible, but like parental choice, this is not overriding.

A new independent Special Needs Tribual is established with a legally qualified chair, to which parents will have a right of appeal if they consider the identification or provision of SEN is inadequate. A new Code of Practice must be produced, which will clearly provide the framework against which the Tribunal will make many of its judgements. The code will, for example, set down time-limits to which assessment and statementing procedures should conform. Schools must give an account, in the governing body's annual report to parents, of their special needs provision and management.

All of this is likely to put SEN higher on the agenda. However, one of the problems since 1981 has been the resource costs of best practice (in fact some practice has evolved precisely to *limit* the

SEN resource drain). The Act provides no new money. Whether it will legally demand a diversion of spending (including teaching time) from other children to SEN pupils, and whether that would be acceptable to the majority of consumers, are questions it fails to answer.

Sections Four and Five

Section Four of the Act re-iterates the law on school attendance, and gives some parents a choice of school even there. Section Five concerns 'failing schools' (ie those deemed to be failing to produce an adequate standard of education by an OFSTED or HMI inspection). In such circumstances, an LEA has the right to appoint additional governors in order to put improvement plans in place. (In the case of GM schools, the Secretary of State can of course simply replace a majority of any GM governing body in these and other circumstances and may regain staffing control by removing delegated powers.) The LEA will, it was said during the passage of the Bill, usually be given a chance to put matters right, but the Secretary of State has the immediate or future option to disband the governing body and call in an Education Association (of at least five members) to remediate faults. A school is deemed to be failing until a later inspection report says otherwise, and once in the hands of an Education Association it will eventually either be wound up or become a GM school.

Final Section

A final miscellaneous section of the Act establishes SCAA in place of SEAC and National Curriculum Council (NCC), insists that LEAs reconvene conferences on their agreed RE syllabus, makes sex education compulsory for schools (but optional for pupils, in that parents may now withdraw children from sex education as well as RE). Primary schools must treat all secondary schools equally regarding the marketing opportunities or distribution of information or literature. LEAs have a duty to provide for all excluded or ill pupils, and pupil exclusion units will form part of such provision. Perhaps most significantly in a symbolic sense, the legal necessity for a separate LEA Education Committee is removed, and perhaps most importantly, in practice, the Secretary of State can direct that both LEAs and funding authorities bring forward plans for extra provision or for the rationalisation of school places according to principles laid down by him. The White Paper repeatedly affirmed the intention to use new powers vigorously in order to reduce surplus places. These powers now exist.

The Act, taken in conjunction with the many regulations that will flow from it, and associated documents such as the SEN Code of Practice, and the Common Funding Formula which the funding authorities will operate, must have a profound effect on the system, both in its particular enactments and in its centralising of powers for future governments to use. Perhaps though, anyone who this year predicts exactly what those effects will be has not understood the Act.

1.2

Management of Health and Safety in Schools

Chris Doak and Joan Atkins

Health and safety management is about the effective control of risks, it is not a 'bolt-on' activity; it is very much at the core of whole school management and needs to be integrated into a wide range of management processes. Many management decisions will have health and safety implications, be they linked to the curriculum, the premises, personnel or finance.

There are very few work activities that create such a broad range of health and safety risks as education. From asbestos to zoo visits the potential for harm comes in myriad forms. The effectiveness of risk control depends on careful planning, the co-operation of all those involved in managing the risks, clear lines of communication and careful monitoring to ensure that control measures continue to be adequate. Failure of this element of the management process can have the most disastrous consequences both in human and financial terms. It is of paramount importance that all involved have a clear idea of what these responsibilities are and what is expected of them. (School management arrangements in Scotland differ somewhat from England and Wales. Scottish school board members should check their responsibilities with their education authority.)

Health and safety responsibilities

In general, health and safety is a shared responsibility between the parties involved in managing the school, be it governors, headteachers, principals, staff, the Local Education Authority (LEA) and in the case of church schools, the diocese. The level of responsibility will relate to the level of control.

Health and safety law is intended to protect both employees and non-employees (including pupils and students) from the risks to their health and safety arising from work activities.

Employers' responsibilities

In law, employers have the main responsibility for health and safety arrangements and in most schools the employer is the LEA. In aided, grant-maintained and most independent schools, the employer is the governing body.

The main responsibilities of employers are:

- to safeguard, as far as is reasonably practicable, the health, safety and welfare of not only their employees but non-employees who may be affected by the work activity, ie pupils, parents, visitors, etc;

- to formulate health and safety policies, procedures and arrangements and to monitor their effectiveness;

- to appoint competent people to assist in carrying out risk assessments and to monitor the effectiveness of control measures.

Although the main duties are placed on employers, both managers, other employees and controllers of premises (eg governors) all have obligations under health and safety law, as do self-employed people. For example, contractors employing school meals and cleaning staff, have employer duties. The school management has a duty to contractors' staff to ensure that they are not put at risk by the condition of the premises. It is important that the school management and contractors liaise and co-operate to ensure the health and safety of all on site.

Employees' duties

These are twofold:

- to take reasonable care of their own health and safety and that of others affected by their acts or omissions at work; and

- to co-operate with their employers in order to permit them to carry out their legal duties.

In schools this means staff should follow the detailed health and safety advice that has been published and circulated to education establishments and internal policies approved by governors and headteachers. They must report any unsafe conditions or practices of which they are aware. The degree of responsibility depends on the extent of management control that is exercised by the individual, hence headteachers and department heads/curriculum leaders will have more control than classroom teachers or technicians and thus more responsibility. Teachers must also consider their common law duties *in loco parentis* for the pupils in their care.

Governors' responsibilities

School governors also have a responsibility for health and safety, the extent of which depends on how much control they have of the management of the school. In voluntary-aided and grant-maintained schools this control is total and they must comply fully with the employers' duties.

For county-controlled schools, under local management (LMS), the LEA remains the employer, but since the governors control most expenditure, in practice they exercise considerable control over health and safety locally. Providing that they act in accordance with the LEA's published policy and guidelines, there should be no difficulty in governors complying with their legal duties.

New regulations

Six European Community health and safety directives were translated into UK law in January 1993. These cover the following areas:

- Management of Health and Safety at Work
- Workplace (Health, Safety and Welfare)
- Display Screen Equipment (VDUs)
- Manual Handling Operations
- Provision and Use of Work Equipment
- Personal Protective Equipment at Work

In the main, these regulations (known affectionately as the six-pack) require an identification and assessment of the risks to the health and safety of employees and non-employees and effective arrangements to be made for planning, organising, monitoring and reviewing the measures implemented to remove or adequately control these risks. More specifically, those responsible for managing schools will need to:

- develop an overall, coherent prevention policy linked to risk assessment;
- write health and safety risk assessments for all processes and work activities;
- appoint competent persons to assist in the above tasks;
- detail requirements on the design and maintenance of the premises to ensure a healthy working environment for staff and pupils;
- consider more detailed emergency procedures;
- increase the provision of information to employees, non-employees and temporary workers;
- increase employee training;
- consult with union-appointed safety representatives;
- meet safety and health requirements for handling loads;
- consider the design, specification and use of VDUs, office equipment, work stations and furniture;
- establish additional requirements for the control of hazardous substances;
- provide more safety signs;
- establish minimum requirements for the provision and use of personal protective equipment;
- consider minimum health and safety requirements for the use of work equipment. These include requirements for maintenance, training, information, stability, controls, guarding of machinery, protection against mechanical failure, etc.

OFSTED inspections

At the same time, OFSTED Inspectors have 'a responsibility to record and report on aspects of the school, whether of provision or practice, which, in the light of the inspection, the judgement of the inspection team and any information provided by the school, constitute a threat to health and safety'. To this end the OFSTED-registered Inspector will:

- comment on any health and safety risks observed during inspection;
- record any health and safety risks observed during inspection;

- record any health and safety irregularities and bring these to the attention of the headteacher and the employer;

- check that the school is aware of the need to comply with statutory requirements for health and safety and has clear procedures to identify and control health and safety risks, including:
  - a written statement of health and safety policy;
  - identification of staff responsible for the implementation and development of policy;
  - arrangements for dealing with accidents and emergencies;
  - procedures for implementing, monitoring and reviewing the arrangements for health and safety – this may cover, for example, the fabric of the building and condition of the electrical supply, as well as the suitability of play and recreational areas;
  - a record of health and safety training of staff for particular responsibilities, eg first aid, use of specified materials and equipment, supervision and teaching of educational activities;
  - a record of any identified health and safety concerns and the action proposed.

Schools' health and safety policy

Apart from being a legal requirement this written policy is the nucleus around which successful risk control can and should be built.

The policy should relate to all school activities that may pose a health and safety risk, whether on or off the premises. Many LEAs have produced a detailed framework for schools to use.

Each school should consider the organisation and arrangements that will best control the risks to which its staff, pupils and visitors, may be exposed. The Health and Safety Executive has suggested the following elements need to be included:

Statement of general policy
This should indicate a clear commitment by the schools management.

Organisation for carrying out the policy
This sets out who is responsible for what throughout the management structure and details lines of communication both within the school and externally.

Arrangements

The arrangements for carrying out the functions allocated to individuals need to be clearly set out. Sources of expert advice and relevant publications should be listed, including codes of safe practice and statutory requirements. The procedures for risk assessment and control together with emergency procedures should the control measures fail, need to be planned and recorded.

Standards of performance relating to these arrangements need to be set which are realistic, achievable and measurable.

Monitoring the policy

The frequency and level of monitoring will vary, depending on the size and complexity of the establishment and the extent of the risks involved.

The aim is to assess whether the policy is being effective and the standards set are being achieved. Apart from this active monitoring, reactive monitoring also needs to take place when things go wrong. Thus we can learn from our mistakes and identify why standards of performance were not met. The information collected via the monitoring process can be used to review the policy and identify ways of improving performance.

Auditing

This is a periodic objective and qualitative assessment of the success of health and safety management best carried out by a suitably qualified and experienced external assessor. This exercise will inform the school management of the suitability, reliability and effectiveness of the systems in place.

In larger schools it is becoming increasingly popular to set up health and safety committees involving headteachers, governors, teachers, non-teaching staff, union representatives, and so on to develop and monitor school policy. It should be noted that the establishment and activities of such committees may be governed by specific legislative requirements. Similarly, union health and safety representatives perform functions related to these regulations on behalf of their members. These functions should be seen as separate from, but complementary to, the management's responsibilities.

Teaching health and safety

If it is accepted that a major contributory factor to the level of risks in schools is the experience (or lack of it) and attitudes of the pupils, then any effort put into making them more safety conscious is time well spent.

There are many techniques and opportunities for integrating health and safety into the curriculum. If the process of risk assessment and control is used as a framework to achieve awareness, pupils will be better placed to cope with the risks they meet as supervision and control is progressively relaxed in the later years of schooling and on into employment. The required level of awareness will not be achieved by blindly following safety rules. Pupils need to be exposed to a strong health and safety culture.

A word of encouragement

Schools should not be overwhelmed by what may appear to be formidable health and safety responsibilities. The education sector has a good record in achieving reasonable standards of health and safety. This is in no small part due to the commitment of a caring management and staff. Many of the policies and arrangements already in place in schools will go a long way to ensuring that this record is maintained. These new regulations and changes in management structure offer a golden opportunity to review existing policy and practice with the aim of improving on the success of health and safety management.

Where can help be found?

Maintained and voluntary-aided schools

Many LEAs have specialist safety advisers who can assist with information, training and advice. These advisers are supported by other specialists for such matters as curriculum, premises and occupational health, to provide a comprehensive support system tailored to the special nature of the education sector. The Diocesan Authority will also assist voluntary-aided schools.

Grant-maintained and independent schools

Grant-maintained and independent schools' associations will be of assistance and some LEAs and private consultants offer a commercial advice service.

Health and safety issues in schools cover a very broad range of topics and there are many sources of information and advice available. It is important that the advice given is appropriate for schools. It is therefore recommended that great care is exercised when using new sources. The Health and Safety Executive (HSE) and the Department For Education (DFE) can assist schools with lists of appropriate publications and addresses of organisations able to offer competent advice.

Outdoor and adventurous activities

This article has attempted to explain the position of health and safety in relation to the general management of the school. Recent experience suggests that a major area of concern relates to the position of governors, headteachers, staff and pupils involved in and organising outdoor activities. The law clearly places considerable responsibility for such activities on governors and headteachers, but provided they have acted reasonably this should not be a cause of concern.

Most LEAs provide clear guidance on outdoor activities in an attempt to minimise the risks involved in activities that, by definition, must have some element of risk attached to them. It is important to ensure that suitably qualified and experienced instructors and appropriate well-maintained facilities and equipment are available in all cases.

The recent tragedy in Lyme Bay which resulted in the deaths of four students has legitimately heightened many people's concerns. Devon County Council, along with many other organisations involved in outdoor education, have called for legislation to protect young people and to ensure an adequate system of inspection and registration of outdoor activity centres.

The Government has yet to accede to this reasonable proposal and therefore individual schools are recommended to check facilities and the supervising organisation very carefully before undertaking outdoor activities that are such an important part of the personal development of the individual student.

Chris Doak and Joan Atkins are Health & Safety Officers with Devon LEA. The authors are writing in a personal capacity and their views are not necessarily those of Devon County Council.

1.3

The Children Act 1989

Ben Whitney

Introduction

The Children Act 1989, which became law in October 1991, is the most wide-ranging reform of the law concerning children this century. As schools are the largest agency working with children, it is vital that school managers are familiar with its contents and philosophy. (See *The Children Act and Schools 'a Guide to Good Practice'*, Kogan Page 1993).

Although education is not the primary focus of the legislation, children's needs must be addressed as a whole. If educational professionals are to play their full part in inter-agency procedures for promoting the welfare of children, and if the rights and responsibilities of parents are to be properly respected, the provisions of the Act must be understood and applied by school staff and governors. There are several specific implications for schools and LEAs which are growing in significance as the Act begins to be worked out in practice.

Key changes

- Family Proceedings Courts replace Juvenile Courts for all welfare/care decisions about children (Youth Courts deal with criminal matters only);

- court intervention in children's lives is to be kept to the minimum required to safeguard their welfare;

- 'custody' and 'access' are replaced by new orders to deal with issues arising from separation/divorce;

- parents retain responsibility for their children even if they are no longer living with them;

- agencies and professionals must treat parents as partners, working with them by agreement wherever possible;

- children must be consulted and involved in decisions which affect their lives;

- the grounds for care proceedings are changed to 'significant harm' rather than specific concepts such as 'moral danger' or absence from school;

- children in larger residential schools and those being cared for away from their parents are given greater protection by regular monitoring, inspection and independent complaints procedures.

There are three main areas with direct implications for school managers:

1. The welfare of the child

This is the paramount concern and central principle of the Act. S27 place a *duty* on local authorities and agencies to work together in helping parents to safeguard and promote the welfare of their children. Where children are defined as 'in need' under S17, services must be made available which support and encourage their parents in caring for them. Children with special educational needs, as well as those with attendance difficulties or at risk of exclusion, could all be included within local 'in need' criteria. LEAs and schools *must* then be active participants in addressing their problems.

Courts will make use of the 'welfare checklist' (S1(3)) when key decisions are needed, to ensure that the child's interests are protected. This list includes a requirement that courts pay attention to a child's 'educational needs'. Reports from school staff may be requested by court welfare officers and social workers in order to help courts obtain all the necessary information.

Child protection

All schools must have a named co-ordinator, responsible for making sure that locally agreed inter-agency procedures are followed. Staff, both teaching and non-teaching, should receive adequate training and senior management should monitor that referrals are dealt with appropriately. More children first disclose abuse to teachers than to any other professional; this responsibility must be recognised and taken seriously. Ensuring that key staff are given full opportunity to participate in case conferences etc. is essential. (For more detail see 'Working Together', DoH, 1991, HMSO)

Listening to children

While only a few schools have formal consultation procedures, it is good practice to ensure that all children have the opportunity to call attention to any problem they may be experiencing in school. Not all children can rely on their parents to act for them. Issues might range from unresolved bullying to racist remarks from fellow pupils or staff. Children are entitled to know that they will be listened to, in addition to the more formal independent investigation that may later be required to verify their complaint.

Children in difficulty

Counsellors with specialist pastoral skills should be available within the school for children experiencing difficulties. Wherever possible, they should draw on the insights of professionals in other agencies who may specialise in particular issues of behaviour, language, disability etc. In situations where relationships at home have broken down, or the family is experiencing particular stress, children may be 'accommodated' by the Social Services Department under S20, either with foster-carers or in a residential unit. These voluntary arrangements must be carefully distinguished from the child who is 'in care' by virtue of a care order under S31. Detailed arrangements concerning the continued involvement of parents at school should be clarified in written agreements wherever possible.

2. *Parental responsibility*

Parents are central to school life. But not all children live in conventional nuclear families. School managers *must* have a clear grasp of the Act's provisions about parental responsibility in order to reflect the reality of children's family circumstances. This legal concept, defined in S3 as 'all the rights, duties, powers, responsibilities and authority which by law a parent has in relation to the child and his property', is immensely important for defining pastoral practice and clarifying the involvement of parents, especially in 'split' families. The following information should be required in admission procedures and updated as appropriate. Only by doing this can a school know who to include as a 'registered parent' under the Education Acts 1944/1993.

A quick guide to parental responsibility (S2ff)

Where actual parents are *married, separated or divorced*, parents have parental responsibility, irrespective of where the child lives. Only adoption removes it (though there may be changes here in future). Both parents should be involved in the child's education wherever possible. The Act has specifically redefined the term 'parent' in education law to include people with parental responsibility living apart from their child as well as those who have care of the child day-to-day (Schedule 13). Data management systems should collect, store and use this information accordingly. Only where there are specific restrictions imposed on parents should their involvement be curtailed. Most will not be in this position, even after divorce.

Where parents are unmarried, only the mother has parental responsibility, unless the father has obtained it by agreement or order. It is essential that schools are aware of whether a child's father actually has legal responsibility for him/her. If not, key decisions, especially the giving of authority to the school on admission, for trips etc, should be made only by the mother wherever possible. Only those with parental responsibility can arrange for others to carry it out on their behalf.

Where a child is living with people other than his/her actual parents, (foster-carers, step parents, other relatives etc), school staff must check carefully whether these people have obtained parental responsibility for him/her. They are 'parents' but they will not normally have 'parental responsibility'; this may lie with someone else living apart from the child. Simply caring for the child does not necessarily give a person the right to make decisions on the child's behalf. Forms may need amendment to make this clear. References to 'parent or guardian' are now out of date. It should be 'parent' for general use or 'person with parental responsibility' when the exercise of authority is required. 'Guardianship' is a specific status, normally affecting only the very few children whose parents are dead.

Court orders

Information must also be obtained about whether there are any court orders which affect the child and his/her parents. These might be 'public' law orders (such as care orders or orders for child protection), or, far more commonly, 'private' law orders, normally made in the context of separation/divorce etc (S8). Unlike procedures before the Children Act, orders will not be made unless they are needed, but if they are made, they must define pastoral practice accordingly.

The four new 'Section 8' orders are:

- *residence orders* (not 'custody'), which define where a child must live, give parental responsibility to anyone named as living with him/her, (in addition to anyone who has it already) and prevent the child being known by a new surname without consent from all those with parental responsibility for him/her;

- *contact orders* (not 'access'), which define a child's right to contact with parents and others;

- *prohibited steps orders* which place restrictions on normal rights to exercise parental responsibility; and

- *specific issue orders* which resolve particular disputes about the welfare of the child such as which school he/she should attend or questions of religious practice.

Only orders can be used as the basis for restricting parental involvement. Otherwise school managers must ensure that all persons with parental responsibility are treated equally wherever possible regarding ballots, consultations, information, reports etc.

3. Absence from school

The Children Act has introduced the education supervision order (S36) as an additional means of helping children and their parents where there have been significant problems with school attendance. Applications can be made only by the LEA through the education welfare/social work service. These proceedings are not punitive, and a child can no longer be placed on a care order due to non-attendance.

Orders, which last initially for one year, enable a nominated supervisor to 'advise, assist and befriend' the child and his/her parents and to give 'directions' if required to ensure that the child is properly educated. Consultation must first take place with the Social Services Department to ensure that no other provision is more appropriate. ESOs are comparatively rare, though when made, full involvement by school staff is essential if the LEA's action is to be successful.

More frequently, the principles of the Children Act about partnership and agreements will form the basis of how to deal with unauthorised absence from school. As elsewhere, courts will only be used when needed and when all voluntary means have been tried. Children commit no offence by staying away, so, where children rather than parents are the focus of the problem, responses must be based on trying to help them to change their behaviour rather than seeking sanctions against them. Parents, EWOs/ESWs, other agencies, schools, and children themselves should aim to work together within a context which promotes and safeguards the child's welfare. Such an approach requires an openness to negotiation and compromise in both practice and policy if it is to be effective.

Conclusion

It should be a clearly defined management responsibility to ensure that all these provisions are reflected in day-to-day school life as required, so that the welfare of children at school can be adequately safeguarded. Key staff, governors, committees and working groups must make sure that they are operating with full knowledge of the Act. Good practice should ensure that we end up with well-protected, better adjusted children and more responsive and involved parents. That must be in everyone's interests.

KOGAN PAGE

Part Two

Whole School Management Planning

Radioactive waste disposal.
3 ways to explain it.

UK Nirex has three teachers' packs aimed at the secondary school level. These ready-made class projects can be used to complement the Science, Geography and Technology curricula.

Safe for the Future

For 14-16 year olds, focused on the science curriculum, and includes interactive computer software, work cards, posters and comprehensive teachers notes.

The Technology of Radioactive Waste Disposal

Designed for 11-16 year olds studying technology and includes six wall charts, a teachers' booklet with fact sheets and a video.

Safe Today, Safe Tomorrow

A joint science/geography pack for 11-13 year olds. Includes the discovery and uses of radiation and the processes involved in choosing a radioactive waste disposal site.

We also offer a range of other educational and information resources including posters, videos, fact sheets and brochures.

2.1

Values, Vision And Leadership

Howard Green

Are 'management' and 'leadership' the same thing?

Most definitions of 'management' are focused on people and tasks. For example, the School Management Task Force proposed that management was achieving goals by, with and through people. The Industrial Society, which has extensive experience of management training, describes the purposes of management as developing individuals, building teams and achieving tasks.

Hughes (1987) has written about the leadership of professionally-staffed organisations like schools and hospitals. He accepts the importance of the manager sub-role but also underlines, for those in education, the equal importance of the educator sub-role, exemplified by the title 'head teacher'. The challenge for educational leadership since the advent of local management has been to hold the educator and the manager sub-roles in creative tension. For many heads, the manager sub-role has predominated and there has been very little time left for educational leadership – a potentially disastrous situation.

But why these words of alarm? Recent research on organisational (rather than team) leadership has made it clear that the formulation of values and vision is central to success. The Biblical adage 'without vision the people perish' has been applied in a new context where phrases like 'ethical leadership' and 'transformational leadership' have now subsumed narrower task-focused terms like 'situational leadership'.

Organisational leaders should be seeking answers to questions like 'why are we in business at all?'; 'how do we want to operate as an organisation?'; and 'where are we heading?'

Those in senior positions should make time to stand back and view the wood, not get continually caught up among the trees. This is not an ivory-tower view of leadership, as senior staff must still be seen at the grass-roots of the organisation, but it does help to establish the priorities on the agendas of those in leadership positions.

To answer the rhetorical question used as the heading for this section, management and leadership are not the same thing. Management is primarily about working with individuals and teams to achieve tasks, while leadership has as its focus the identification and articulation of corporate values and the implementation of an organisation's vision for the future through strategic planning.

Does the team think?

All teams, but particularly senior teams, need to make time for thinking and planning. It may be easier to consume all the team's energy on the nuts and bolts of running a school like curriculum planning, budgeting and staff development, but if the senior staff do not undertake the sometimes difficult evaluation, review and long-term planning, then nobody else will do these crucial tasks. Nor is it time wasted to reflect on issues of philosophy, values, purpose and vision.

Education has been driven for too long by utilitarian pressures, and there is an urgent need to step aside from this onward rush to ask some fundamental questions like 'what are schools for?' and, more specifically, 'what does this school stand for?' The debate should include governors, parents and pupils as well as staff. It may be a threatening debate because we shall be opening ourselves to criticism and we may have to do things differently in the future; change is often an uncomfortable process. However, if change is openly discussed and has wide ownership, then the organisation will be stronger as a result. There will be enormous satisfaction (even celebration) as the strategic plan unfolds.

Pedler et al (1991) have researched a wide range of successful organisations in the UK (including schools) and concluded that the best are 'learning companies'. They regularly go through the processes described above, involving all the main stakeholders in review and development towards a shared vision of what the company wants to achieve. Here a 'company' is defined as any group of people involved in a particular activity or enterprise.

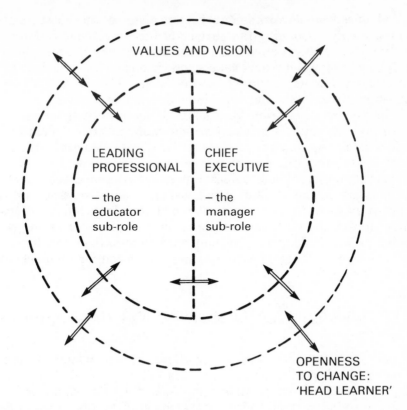

Figure 2.1.1 *Aspects of the school leader*

Figure 2.1.1 summarises the main aspects of the school leader outlined above. The inter-connecting arrows indicate that the various aspects are closely related and constantly interacting.

Values and vision – the triggers for the School Development Plan

Now that schools are locally-managed and have direct responsibility for most of their budgets, it is vital that they use a much more sophisticated approach to development planning. Hargreaves & Hopkins (1991) have written a very clear and concise account of this important process. They show how the development planning process leads from the aims of the school (which are expressions of its values and vision) through specific plans for the curriculum, staffing, staff development, finance etc, on to the daily life of the school and, finally, to its main outcome – pupil achievement.

Evidence from government inspectors suggests that most schools are still only scratching the surface of the development planning process and that, in particular, far too little time is spent on the crucial first step of defining values and vision and turning them into a clear set of aims or targets for the future. They miss the initial question, 'what is the purpose of our development plan?'

Further evidence from West's (1993) research with heads and governors shows that schools are not confident about identifying and articulating values and a vision for the future despite the fact that local communities want this to happen and that there is still much to play for. Where values and vision are concerned, there is often a deafening silence during senior team discussions or at governors' meetings. Time must be made available for this crucial first step in the development planning process and training provided to help heads and governors with the process of identifying, articulating and implementing values and vision for their schools.

The challenge of making values and vision explicit

If one needs any more convincing about the importance of taking time to establish a framework of values and vision for the future of a school, (of exercising positive organisational leadership), government inspection should provide the imperative. Many years ago HMI (1977) published a brief document, 'Ten Good Schools'. On a regional basis, HMIs had identified the best secondary schools in their areas and they had then teased out the qualities that these schools had in common. The final section of the document says this:

> 'What (the schools) all have in common is effective leadership . . . they take trouble to make their philosophies explicit for themselves and to explain them to parents and pupils; the foundation of their work and corporate life is an acceptance of shared values.' p36

These words still apply although schools now face a rather different approach from government inspectors, co-ordinated by the newly formed Office for Standards in Education. The criteria for inspection are much more explicit and include pupils' spiritual, moral, social and cultural development, including their behaviour. The National Curriculum Council paper on spiritual and moral development notes that one of the main contributors to these aspects of development is the ethos of the school. Questions of values and vision can be ducked no longer!

Block (1987) mentions three notes of warning for those in positions of leadership as they begin to make the school's values explicit and articulate a vision. First in an implicit way, articulating our vision for the future signifies a disappointment with what exists now. This will undoubtedly upset some of the current stakeholders in the school. Second, expressing our vision exposes the future that we wish for our school and opens us up to potential conflict with the visions of other people. At the outset we must decide which aspects of our vision are open for negotiation and which are non-negotiable. Third, articulating a vision for the future forces us to hold ourselves accountable for acting in a way that is congruent with that vision – we must actually do what we say we do!

Conclusion

Successful school management must be set in the context of effective leadership. That effectiveness is rooted in clear values and a vision for the future which, as far as possible, are owned by the whole school community and made explicit. The values and vision do not remain 'pie in the sky' but are converted into a development plan and should be seen day by day in all aspects of school life.

Further reading

Block P (1987) *The Empowered Manager*, Jossey Bass.
Hargreaves D H and Hopkins D (1991) *The Empowered School*, Cassell.
HMI (1977) *Ten Good Schools*, HMSO.
Hughes M, Ribbins P and Thomas H (1987) *Managing Education: The System & the Institution*, Cassell.
Pedler M, Burgoyne J and Boydell T (1991) *The Learning Company*, McGraw Hill.
West S (1993) *Educational Values for School Leadership*, Kogan Page.

The School Development Plan
Bill Berry

Past imperfect!

The whole process of planning for the future based on the experiences of the past and an assessment of the present is certainly not new. If you take the trouble to dig through the school's archives, you will doubtless find some dusty document entitled 'The Way Forward' or 'The Next Five Years' which would be the equivalent of what we now call an 'Institutional or School Development Plan'.

Rather than creating a document as a public relations exercise to comfort the occasional querying parent or governor, today the planning process is much more refined. We have a clearer view of what we want our plans to achieve and how to assess these achievements.

In the midst of such bewildering , time changings we must reflect on what a school is currently doing and consider what a school needs to do if it is to keep up with and manage necessary development. A school development plan is the key.

Be purposeful!

At the outset, it is essential that the development plan is not just seen as yet another initiative imposed by some ambitious manager who wishes to make a mark. The motive for the plan must be based on a desire to be pro-active rather than re-active and a desire to create a guide-rail through the fog of current uncertainties and the plethora of recent changes.

The purpose of the plan should be clearly defined for all those who will be part of its creation and all those whom it will affect. The basic structure of the plan itself should certainly contain the following:

- an assessment of where the school is now;

- a recognition of changes which are needed;

- a plan of the path of change and an assessment of resource implications;

- a means for evaluating the success of the agreed changes.

A group of professionals should be brought together to clarify the direction of development within the context of the school's stated aims and objectives. This group will form the bedrock of the entire planning process.

Planning in practice

There are many routes that can be taken in the production and implementation of a school development plan; the steps below are not in any way definitive. They should, however, give some guidelines for what can be a lengthy and sensitive process.

Step 1 – Planning the calendar

A small group, perhaps a senior team, should schedule the production of the plan so there is some idea of the time span covering all stages.

Step 2 – Outline of contents

An outline of potential contents must be produced before there is any attempt to put flesh on the bones. Headings for this list of development areas will almost certainly contain: curriculum development, finance and resource planning, staffing structure, assessment and recording, external links, evaluation.

Step 3 – Fleshing the bones

Items from the above list of contents should be taken by individual members of the senior staff for 'fleshing out'. The work should be based on statements of where the school is now and suggested plans for the future. It can prove useful to involve an adviser or governor at this stage who could formulate plans for the evaluation section.

Step 4 – First introductions

This is the time to introduce the skeletal first draft to the whole staff and begin to involve others in its production. There is enough in place to make its purpose clear to colleagues and to establish a style. At this point it is essential to 'sell' the plan as that guide-rail which will help to make sense of a welter of initiatives and changes rather than being yet another burden for war-weary colleagues.

Step 5 – Close consideration

Hard on the heels of the introduction should be a chance for a full staff debate, offering the opportunity for criticism of what has been written as well as suggestions for additions. Ideally, this debate should take place during a training day. If the introduction has created a positive backdrop for the plan, it is likely that there will be many suggestions for additions or at least a refinement of the original headings.

This is an opportunity to involve a wider group of staff in the creation of the plan, as individuals or groups are asked to write sections of the document along the lines of the original outline structure.

Step 6 – Draft audit

All these contributions to the document sit together as an 'audit' of the school providing a view of the direction it should take. This completed first draft should be presented to staff for consideration and, following discussions, a priority list should be drawn up so that a realistic set of tasks can be planned within a manageable period of time.

Even if some areas are not seen to be urgent for development in the short term, it is essential that all sections of the audit are shown to be a valuable part of an analytical exercise.

Step 7 – Action plan

However well produced, it is unlikely that the audit document will be a manageable tool for action since it is almost certain to be too long and too broad in scope. It is therefore important that a brief, pithy and effective action plan is teased out of the audit – to be used as a checklist for individuals, departments and task groups and as a short-term guide for action and evaluation.

This action plan will contain the plans for development within a variety of areas as well as the identification of the key players in that development. Ideally, it should be no more than a few sides of A4 and should not be trammelled with any analysis. At this stage it is important to assess the financial implications of each section of the plan so that a judgement can be made on the feasibility of the programme and priorities can be adjusted as necessary.

Step 8 – Publication

Time must be given to the final introduction of the audit and action plan. As noted before, the value of the work done on the audit must be stressed publicly while recognising the more practical nature of the slimmer action plan.

Upon publication, attention must be drawn to the responsibilities of groups and individuals to put the plan into action with an emphasis on the need for *all* to both 'own' and contribute to the process of implementation. The status of the two documents can be enhanced in a number of ways: by presenting the development plan to governors and parents; by making frequent reference to it at planning meetings; by involving the advisory service in its implementation and evaluation; by making available the two documents in the staffroom and governors' library so that they can be referred to and consulted by all staff and visitors.

Step 9 – Evaluation

The process of evaluation will be a constant one as groups and individuals reach, or at least move towards, an identified goal. However, it is important to use the action plan as a means of praise before the whole cycle of analysis and planning starts once again. There is nothing like a generous use of the oil of self congratulation before the engine starts to turn afresh!

Time must be set aside at staff and governors' meetings to assess progress towards targets set as well as to identify continuing priorities or new areas of development.

Step 10 – Audit again?

It is not practical to attempt a full audit of the school and its priorities each year, but it remains essential that an action plan is produced so that there are clear aims in place for all to use. Once the planning cycle is in place there is the need for regular tuning but only an occasional overhaul. It is likely that an audit could only be attempted every three years or so.

If the process of OFSTED inspections continues on the proposed calendar, then the familiar pattern of auditing, action planning and budgeting could look like Figure 2.2.1.

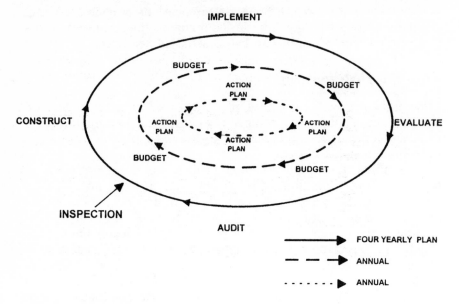

Figure 2.2.1 *SDP planning cycle*

Principles for success

The steps above can be adapted or passed over if seen to suit a particular school, but Table 2.2.1 gives a few principles that are essential prerequisites for successful development planning.

If school development planning is managed well, a wide range of benefits will be seen:

- a welding together of the staff group;
- an involvement of the governing body in the planning process;
- a sense of direction and achievement for all; and
- an affirmation of the school's aims and objectives.

But whatever the benefits in these areas and others, they will seem paltry if the main principle and purpose of development planning is not achieved. No one must be allowed to lose sight of the fact that the development and enhancement of children's learning is at the heart of the whole process.

---

1. Prepare the calendar of production for the audit and action plan with care and keep to deadlines.

2. Involve *all* staff at any early stage and maintain that involvement through each stage of the process. A feeling of *ownership* of the plan, and involvement in its development, implementation and evaluation is essential.

3. Emphasise the 'guidance' offered by the completed development plan and stress that it will ease the process of change rather than add to its burden.

4. Keep the printed outcomes manageable so that there is the chance for easy reference and evaluation. A large tome of detailed analysis will never be referred to, while a slimmer volume could be a living and working document.

5. At every stage of development, emphasise the central purpose of the exercise, that the school development plan is created to improve the learning of students.

Table 2.2.1 *Principles of successful development planning*

Further reading

Holly, P and Southworth, G *The Developing School.*
Planning for School Development 1 DFE.
Planning for School Development 2 DFE.

Quality Assurance in Schools

John West-Burnham

Quality assurance is a central concept in the effective management of any organisation. In essence it is concerned with systems, documentation and procedures which ensure that all products and services conform to a predetermined specification.

Central to the concept is the definition of quality. Traditionally, quality has been defined as goodness, truth or beauty. It is clearly impossible to set up a system which is designed to guarantee goodness; it is too elusive a concept to be managed. Quality assurance depends on a fundamentally different view of quality, ie that quality consists in meeting the requirements, specifications or needs of a customer or client. For many organisations this represents a culture shift away from 'we know what quality is' to 'your requirements are our only definition of quality'.

In schools, quality exists in meeting the actual needs of clients – children, their parents, other schools, the Local Education Authority (LEA), the National Curriculum Council (NCC), HMCI etc, and not in a vague notion of 'the educated child' which is the monopoly of the professionals.

Quality assurance moves the culture of an organisation away from control and power relationships towards a recognition of the trust, responsibility and authority that every employee is entitled to if they are to work effectively. Thus, the concept facilitates the movement from dependence to interdependence.

Quality assurance versus quality control

These terms are often thought of as being synonymous; in fact they represent different approaches to managing quality. In essence, quality control is historic, reactive and based on power, while quality assurance is based on prevention and seeks to define requirements in advance to minimise the possibility of a product or service not conforming to the specification. Control leads to waste, scrapping and reworking. Assurance seeks to create the situation where 'right first time' is a real possibility.

Most schools work on inspection. Assessment procedures, by and large, are a form of inspection. Children are not given the assessment criteria and therefore, by definition, it is impossible for them to get it right. The quality control approach has some significant psychological implications – it works by failure, by denying the possibility of getting it right. Equally significantly, control institutionalises waste – it presumes scrap. This is easy to see in a manufacturing organisation where up to 25 per cent of raw materials may end up being scrapped. The introduction of a quality assurance approach can reduce this to five per cent or less. The difference is in lost profits, excessive costs and, crucially, customer satisfaction. The 'Friday car' is a classic example of quality control.

It may be difficult to establish a direct correlation in schools with the 'Friday car', however, the following are symptomatic of the same problem:

• homework instructions that are not understood;

• meetings that do not reach a decision;

• messages that are not passed on;

• letters that have to be re-typed;

• reports that are not self-explanatory;

• deadlines that are not met.

These are not inevitable 'accidents' of organisational life; they are deliberate and avoidable waste. Many managers in schools will spend much of their time reworking, correcting, putting right. Every time something has to be repeated it represents a diversion from the key purpose of the school – children's learning.

Quality assurance systems

Every school publishes (perhaps unknowingly) sophisticated quality assurance systems, for example:

• syllabuses and schemes of work;

• safety regulations in the laboratory;

- options schemes;
- school rules;
- financial procedures.

The issue is the extent to which these approaches are based on customer needs, are applied consistently and apply to the totality of school life. As long as there is variation there cannot be quality; if quality is defined as meeting customer needs, then a failure to meet those needs rules out the existence of quality.

Quality assurance therefore requires three elements to be managed:

- the definition of quality;
- the system to assure quality;
- the measurement of compliance.

The definition of quality

The definition is the joint responsibility of supplier and customer. It is for the customer to define the specification with reference to, for example:

- intended usage;
- required outcomes;
- cost;
- standards;
- quantity, etc.

It is for the supplier to clarify the definition, propose enhanced standards and confirm ability to supply. This applies as much to lesson design and resources as it does to a cleaning contract. Suppliers provide a quality service by helping customers to articulate precise requirements. For example, the school asks parents how a consultation evening is best organised, the school management team (SMT) asks subject leaders how they can be best supported.

The system to assure quality

Effective management for quality requires organisations to set up various systems and processes, including those for:

- helping in definition and specification;

- checking;

- using appropriate documentation;

- keeping records;

- designating individual responsibility for ensuring quality.

The management of INSET is a useful example of how such an approach might work in practice. Each of the factors identified above can be replicated in a well-managed staff development programme, by:

- using appraisal as the basis for needs analysis;

- using review, monitoring and feedback;

- using the appraisal statement and INSET policy;

- tracking completion of targets and using career progression profiles;

- providing job descriptions which specify responsibility for managing the development of colleagues.

The measurement of compliance

The measurement of compliance can be carried out in a number of ways, both quantitative and qualitative. Measurement may be objective or based on clients' perceptions – both are valid as indications of conformity. Measurement of a holiday might include reference to punctuality of flight times, accuracy of the brochure description and cost. However, the perception of a 'good' holiday is also important. An SMT meeting can be measured in terms of punctuality in starting and finishing, completion of the agenda etc, but it is also important to measure perceived satisfaction. The quantified evaluation of INSET days can be transferred to school procedures.

Conformity to specification can only be established through measurement. Marking children's work can be used as a measure of teaching effectiveness; response rates to invitations to consultation evenings might say more about the approachability of the school than about parental attitudes.

Setting up quality assurance

As indicated above, most schools will have sophisticated quality assurance systems for many aspects of the school's life. The critical issue is one of comprehensiveness across the school and consistency over time. In order to achieve these elements a number of practical steps can be taken:

1. A clear public commitment to quality in the mission statement and a policy for managing quality.

2. A quality manual (the staff handbook?) which outlines the specific components of how the school will manage quality.

3. A clear definition of the responsibility of every individual to deliver quality to every client on every occasion.

4. The development of 'contracts' to confirm the mutual obligations of supplier and customer.

5. The establishment of 'standard operating procedures' (schemes of work, marking schemes etc) to help deliver consistency.

6. The use of quality audits to establish the integrity of provision against specification. (Internal review and increasingly, preparing for HMCI inspections the 'Framework for Inspection'; is a customer specification.)

ISO 9000/BS 5750

Many of the principles of quality assurance described above are derived from BS 5750, sometimes referred to by its international designation, ISO 9000. In effect this is a 'kite mark' for quality management obtained through the accreditation of an organisation's management systems against specified criteria.

A small number of schools and an increasingly large number of FE Colleges are now being awarded BS 5750 registration. The reported benefits include a detailed analysis of every aspect of the school's work, external advice and support, clear guidelines on what needs to be done (but not how it should be done) and perhaps most significantly, a clearer sense of shared understanding developed through the work involved in preparing for registration.

There is no disputing the validity of these outcomes, however, they are not unique to BS 5750. Much the same benefits have been reported by schools preparing for an OFSTED inspection and using the 'Framework for Inspection' as the basis of a collaborative approach to improvement. The award of the kite mark is undoubtedly significant in marketing terms but its relevance remains questionable. No school has yet published detailed costings (money *and* time) of what it took to achieve registration, not to mention the opportunity cost.

Most worrying is the culture created by BS 5750 which can produce a sense that 'We have got it right, defined it and now all we have to do is deliver'. This is very much at odds with a central principle of quality management – the notion of continuous improvement. There is a danger that BS 5750 might be perceived as evidence of having 'achieved quality' and thereby diminish the drive to improve. The notion of conformity to the quality manual could inhibit the commitment to improvement through learning and thereby diminish personal responsibility. BS 5750 is useful if it is seen as a component of Total Quality and not an end in itself. In the final analysis, BS 5750 is concerned with conformity; there is no guarantee of quality.

'Investors In People'

'Investors In People' (IIP) is another form of externally validated quality assurance, but, unlike ISO 9000, it focuses entirely on the people in the organisation and its commitment to their development. IIP publishes a national standard which is administered through the local Training and Enterprise Councils (TECs). The standard has four principles:

1. A commitment from senior management to develop all employees.

2. A systematic and regular review of the training and development needs of all employees.

3. A clear strategy to train and develop individuals throughout their employment.

4. Regular evaluation of the investment in training and development to monitor effectiveness and plan for the future.

The most cursory examination of IIP will reveal many close parallels between the requirements and the practical application of the School Teacher Appraisal Regulations in LEAs and schools. As with ISO 9000, there are real advantages in responding to external criteria and having to demonstrate that aspiration is matched by action. External accreditation can send a message to the wider community, but, perhaps more importantly, it demonstrates commitment within the organisation. Much of the apprehension about appraisal could be dispelled if it was set in the context of IIP. It also seems highly appropriate for schools to demonstrate in a tangible way their belief in life-long training and development.

The experience of schools and colleges with IIP has generally been very positive. The implementation of IIP guidelines has been found to be directly relevant to the OFSTED crtieria for effective management. The element of IIP that has created the most difficulty has been the involvement of non-teaching staff in all aspects of training and development. In contrast to BS 5750, involvement in IIP appears to be relatively unproblematic and positively advantageous in a number of significant areas of school management.

Conclusion

Quality assurance is about prevention, about using management time and energy to ensure the delivery of quality – right the first time and every time. Anything less cannot be acceptable in the management of children's learning. Quality assurance translates quality from an abstract ideal to a set of real, practical and tangible actions, ensuring that that which is required is delivered. The responsibility of management in schools is to define the standard, to provide the resources and skills, and to measure and improve.

Further reading

Bowring-Carr C and West-Burnham J 1994 *Managing Quality in Schools Workbook*, Longman.
Dale and Plunkett (1990) *Managing Quality*, Philip Allan.
Freeman R 1993 *Quality Assurance in Training and Education*, Kogan Page.
Jenkins HO 1991 *Getting it Right*, Basil Blackwell.
Lessem R 1991 *Total Quality Learning*, Basil Blackwell.
McDonald and Pittott 1990 *Global Quality*, Mercury.
Oakland JS 1993 *Total Quality Management*, Heinemann.
West-Burnham J 1992 *Managing Quality in Schools*, Longman.

2.4

Managing School Inspection

Trevor Yates

Introduction

The OFSTED arrangements are so detailed that there can be no
excuse for any school which is not fully prepared. It is therefore
incumbent on every headteacher to ensure that the whole school is
prepared and ready when the inspector comes to call.

As a first step, revisit *The Handbook for Inspection of Schools*[1] –
Part 2, The Framework and identify exactly how the process will
impact on your school during the three phases of pre-inspection,
inspection and post-inspection.

- review the framework;
- prepare the whole school
  - pupils, staff, governors, parents and local community
  - as individuals
  - as team members.

Pre-inspection

Review the Code of Conduct for Inspectors, which highlights the
roles of individuals and teams and identifies the following key
terms:

1. Information – required by the inspectors before and during the
   inspection.

2. Judgement Recording statements (JRs) – judgements made and recorded by the inspectors.

3. Evidence – collected by the inspectors to support their findings.

4. Indicators – selected items of qualitative data which help in the valuation of quality and standards.

5. The Pre-Inspection Contextual School Indicator (PICSI) Report – set of data provided by Ofsted used to inform inspection judgements.

Ensure that you have sight of the PICSI report and provide as much additional information as possible to set your school in context.

Statutory basis

Ensure that this section is given full and careful consideration. The inspectors will wish to see that every school is meeting its full statutory requirement and has developed all statutory policies. In addition to the more obvious ones, such as the Collective Act of Worship, do not miss out on those that are hidden away eg 5.2 Behaviour and Discipline '. . . designated staff should be properly trained . . . .'
This leads to questions such as:

• Who is your designated member of staff?

• What training have they undertaken?

One suggestion is to keep all DFE circulars in one file for ease of reference.

Lesson observation

Teachers may well feel extremely nervous concerning lesson observation. Ensure that all staff have the opportunity to study the Lesson Observation Proforma and fully understand the grading system.

Parents

Although heads can now introduce them, the parent's meeting and parent's questionnaire still give rise for concern in some schools. Build up your own evidence of parental support through on-going surveys which can be presented to the inspectors.

Paperwork

Many of the forms are extremely simplistic and therefore difficult to complete. Probably even more worrying is how the inspectors then interpret the data, eg comparative information on average Pupil Teacher Ratio which is taken from The Audit Commission Reports – Adding Up the Sums.[2]

Be patient and keep accurate records.

Evidence

The inspectors will only see a *snapshot* of school life. Therefore, one of the main management tasks is to collate and present as much supportive information as possible. Consider creating a 'Portfolio of Evidence' covering every aspect of school life. It may take the form of press cuttings, a yearbook or a set of display boards.

- present all information in the clearest way possible, eg tables and graphs;

- point out the long-term picture, eg large cash injections which distort snapshot figures;

- collect evidence from other sources, eg travel to work unemployment statistics;

- take the opportunity to point out special features, eg community education.

Inspection

The first problem is where to put the inspectors. The more welcome they feel, the better the rapport. Prepare pupils and staff for the feeling of being *swamped* – the inspectors can appear to be everywhere.

Daily briefing meetings with the Registered Inspector are essential to the smooth running of the inspection.

Appoint a *liaison officer* – there is a great deal to be said for delegating this task to a member of the senior management team (SMT) eg deputy head curriculum. Also consider appointing duty officers – members of the SMT – to be available every period to deal with the inspector's queries and staff concerns as they arise.

Be aware that some staff, while finding the lesson observation to be relatively painless, find individual meetings with the inspectors to be extremely harrowing. Ensure that everyone who comes into contact with the inspection team is aware of the risk of provocative or casual comments, which can easily be taken out of context or misinterpreted. Do not attempt to hide things. One of the strengths of a good school with supportive staff and a sensitive SMT is its ability to respond to such instances. Talk them through while the inspection team is still present and misunderstandings can be rectified – once they have left it is too late.

Above all it is essential that SMT keeps its finger on the pulse.

Checklist

- appoint liaison officer;
- develop procedures for emergencies;
- appoint duty officers;
- identify any potential trouble spots;
- create space each day for the SMT to monitor and review.

Post-inspection

Expect a state of numbness to set in; it will take time for things to return back to normal.

Prepare the SMT and governors to receive the initial feedback; and remember that the report does not have to be presented to the full governing body. It is imperative that the head is free to concentrate on listening to the report and is available to correct any factual errors. There are usually one or two errors, often minor but potentially critical. Also encourage governors and colleagues to listen. Stress the importance of unity and that this is not the time to start questioning the inspectors over the judgements which they have made.

Checklist

- Review Handbook – Part 9 – Inspection Reports;
- avoid trying to minute the whole meeting;
- delegate individual members of the SMT to record key points;
- refrain from entering into discussion.

Agree the course of action following the final publication of the report. One very helpful technique is to go through the written report with three different highlight pens (green – strengths/yellow – neutral/red – weaknesses). These comments can then be collected together to form the basis of the press release and draft action plan.

Use the LEA Press Officer, who usually provides clear advice and can obtain quotes from the Chief Education Officer and the Chairman of the Education Committee.

Checklist

• Highlight strengths;

• identify weaknesses;

• produce draft action plan;

• identify who is going to address specific issues;

• prepare press release.

References

1 *Handbook for the Inspection of Schools* (1993) Office For Standards in Education, London: HMSO.
2 *Adding up the Sums: Schools' Management of their Finances* (1993), Audit Commission, Local Government Report No 6, London: HMSO. *Adding up the Sums 2: Comparative Information for Schools* (1993), Audit Commission, Local Government Report No 7, London: HMSO.

Size Doesn't Matter! ... or, Managing Secondary and Primary Schools – Is it the Same Thing?

John Curtis-Rouse

Still no staff college!

Headteachers manage budgets of millions and hundreds of staff. Financial delegation in the 1988 Education Act aimed 'to empower schools to use their closer knowledge of pupils and their communities in determining how resources could be applied to greatest effect.'[1] With uneven and incomplete national provision of management training, it is worth considering if the tasks and necessary competences of primary–secondary management are capable of being addressed together.

In all phases the key functions of management – and leadership – are constant. Equally important *for the individual pupil*, is the quality of the education that the management achieves. A big school is just a conglomeration of more individuals, each as, but no more, important to his/her parents than the child in a tiny infants school.

Managing policy

Two factors have meant that even schools arriving at delegation in the last cohorts have already been blooded in the demands of local management.

First, experiences of schools in earlier cohorts will have provided useful lessons – and probably, however unfairly, some amusement. We all know of the lordly, nearby school that grasped financial delegation, spent £10,000 on new prospectuses and then noticed that its crest was printed in reverse – along with the Latin motto. But often there has been co-operation between schools in and across phases, whether based on formal academic councils, or on looser confederations of collegial headteachers.

Second, national directives have led all heads and governors into difficult but unavoidable local decision-making. On the rollercoaster of assessment at Key Stages 1–3 in 1993, primary heads, with greater experience of managing mutating schemes were possibly better able to maintain a calm and orderly curriculum than some of their secondary colleagues. Appraisal is another initiative that has helped develop local management.

Double or drop

The primary headteacher, with one (teaching) deputy, is less likely to be able to delegate major strategic and planning tasks. A secondary colleague will probably have at least two deputies with significant non-teaching time for management tasks. This focus on the primary head might be seen, of course, as beneficial centralisation – provided that the head doesn't become sick, dispirited or leave!

With the exception of appointing panels, there are as many governors' committees to service in the primary as in the secondary phase. All in all, the primary head is likely to spend more time in policy-forming and review than her/his secondary colleague.

Managing learning and curriculum knowledge

The experience of secondary and primary heads differs in this area more than in any other. Most primary heads will have taught a class for the full teaching week for several years; teaching primary heads still do, despite the 'head's relief' for administration tasks. This brings detailed knowledge of the full curriculum, albeit possibly limited to one year group, and predating National Curriculum (NC). The secondary head will often know a single specialised subject area and must rely for curriculum advice on a broad range of staff.

Secondary heads often envy the curriculum experience of their primary colleagues. Primary heads might wish to do without this envy: the smallest school still needs to teach, assess and record the full phalanx of Core, Foundation, Themes, Skills, Dimensions, RE, RoA and so on.

Empowering the classroom teacher

Every teacher has to manage learning in the classroom. Primary teachers deliver a full curriculum which is undergoing constant change, and their heads have been led by NC and Education Reform Act (ERA) into a degree of empowerment of classroom teachers not seen in many secondary schools, where heads of department make most curriculum decisions.

Managing people – management teams

Every manager wants to assist, praise, support and monitor the work of colleagues. The headteacher too needs such a professional and collaborative 'critical friendship'. Heads need to be sufficiently at ease with their senior colleagues to be able to expect – and accept – the professional and frank appraisal that is a mark of a strong and unified management team.

We are as likely to find a well-defined management team in a medium to large primary school as in secondary schools. Additionally, in primary schools the staff is often small enough for there to be a strong sense of shared purpose, personal valuing and understanding. Communication really is easier in a smaller school.

The individual touch

A school's most valuable/valued resource is its staff. Teachers and support staff place great personal value on time and support given to them personally by the headteacher, especially in a prepared annual interview. The growth of appraisal will affect this perception, but there is evidence that secondary heads are less successful in this vital activity.

Managing resources – support staff

Site Administrator, Maintenance Officer, technicians of all species, Bursar and secretariat . . . with all this panoply of support staff the task of the secondary head must surely be less onerous. However, primary heads often take advantage of the smaller staff and premises they manage to make their budgets cover significant improvements. Small schools of both phases are spared the horrors of Compulsory Competitive Tendering (CCT) and can employ their own cleaners, caretakers and other site staff; many secondary schools are having to deal with imposed 'competitive' contracts that are now failing to provide anything other than headaches.

Nonetheless, specialist staff are free to do the job when it needs to be done; one primary colleague tells me that by the time he is free to chase up site and resources matters, the bank has closed and the builders have all gone home!

Finance

Managing finance is difficult for smaller primary schools. Most employ only one full-time administrative assistant, and the Audit Commission agrees that desirable levels of separation in financial procedure may simply be impossible. The weight of responsibility and accountability upon the head's shouders is thus all the greater.

Primary and secondary heads alike have managed their schools well within uncertain budgets. A 'particular success' of primary school heads is to have increased the level of classroom assistant support by making savings on running costs.[1] The Audit Commission's report[1] at the same time warned that some secondary heads were delegating financial control too widely – the ironic counterpoint to the inability of primary heads to share the burden of running the budget!

Conclusion – structure and leadership

The formal structuring of management will not, in itself, create effective leadership. In both phases there will be examples of

The author is grateful for the assistance of Neville Helme, Headteacher, Callington Primary School, Cornwall, and of Nigel Hughes, Headteacher, Eggbuckland Vale Primary School, Plymouth, in writing this article. The views expressed are the author's own.

wondrous structures of governance and delegation and consultation where there is, sadly, no feeling within the school of *leadership*. Heads have to manage the education of young people, who only have the one life to live; at the same time, they must nurture and further the careers of colleagues, gather and deploy resources and protect the school from undesirable external pressures.

These tasks are not unique to one phase or another; they apply to a university or a nursery unit. Good managers must possess and develop competences whatever their profession, and this is certainly true in education.

Further reading

Audit Commission (1993) *Adding up the Sums*, HMSO.

Audit Commission (1993) *Keeping your Balance*, HMSO.

Bolam, McMahon, Pockington and Weindling (1993) *Effective Management in Schools*, HMSO.

Esp, D (1993) *Competences for School Managers*, Kogan Page.

MacGilchrist and Hall (1993) *Using Management Development Materials*, HMSO.

School Management Task Force (1990) *Developing School Management*, HMSO.

Part Three

Financial Management

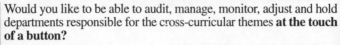

Using IT to manage the cross-curricular themes

The Kirklees PSE Data Manager is a computer program written specifically to enable teachers to manage the five cross-curricular themes and IT and provide a comprehensive, cohesive, progressive and meaningful curriculum for all students. Developed and trialled in Kirklees' schools.

The P.S.E. Data Manager consists of : • a program disc (compatible with any MS DOS machine or Archimedes with a PC emulator) • six photo-copiable user-friendly audit sheets based on NCC guidance • a booklet of instructions.

The Data Manager may be used to record: •host subject •themes and components •when taught •whose responsibility •N C Attainment Targets •lesson description •teaching methods •resources used •skills practised •hours used.

These can then be cross referenced and give the answers to any questions you may have.

3.1

Creating the Annual Budget

Bruce Douglas

What is a budget?

It is 'the expression, in monetary terms, of an institution's plans for a given period, and for given price assumptions'. Contemplation of that typical definition will lead to some very important deductions about budgeting.

First, paradoxical though it may seem, a budget is not about money. Though composed of a list of amounts of money allocated, it is, first and foremost, as the definition says, an expression of *plans*. And those plans are not about money, they are to do with the activities of teaching and learning, and with the personnel, premises, consumables and services required to make these plans happen. The budget is the place where everything is quantified and then costed, but it is the educational activity which drives the budget, not the other way round.

We sometimes pretend the opposite in order to emphasise that we could plan more ambitiously if better resourced, but lack of money does create real educational restraints. Indeed one of our roles as heads and deputies (who else has the authoritative knowledge to perform it?) is to state good reasons why we need more for young people's education. But when we sit down to write a budget, asking for more is not in our minds. Deciding what educational activities can and will happen, certainly is. Educational budgeting is an educationally creative task, unless we choose to describe 'budgeting' as only that final part of the process where educational planning has already taken place, the curriculum has been decided, the staff allocated, and all that is left is to calculate how much exactly the listed teachers, rooms and supplies will cost.

That is a large enough task, and budgeting usually ends there. But the wider definition does hold the important truth that the choices individual teachers or departments make, whether out of educational conviction, through a wider consensus, or in response to institutional or national requirements, are choices which ultimately produce the budget.

So all such decisions – eg the introduction of drama instead of home economics; the abandonment of drama in favour of science; the buying of scientific instruments instead of tennis nets; the replacement of tennis nets instead of computers – which are the stuff of school development, are daily, weekly, yearly, the budget. All are subject to the educational visions (and the power games) that schools contain. Therefore, those who make those decisions really 'control' the budget.

In a profession like teaching, where collegiality is a way of life, it is perhaps as well to remind ourselves and others that the new emphasis on institutional costing that Local Management of Schools (LMS) has created is not necessarily a threat to that tradition.

Not that there is therefore an easy, sentimental way of creating a budget which everybody owns. A professional consensus, and a consensus between professional and lay bodies (especially the governing bodies), is generally largely in place (ie mostly schools agree that most of what they do is right). But the professional debate is splendidly ferocious at the margin, and lay-professional togetherness has to be won through explanation, two-way listening, mutual respect and compromise.

Budgets really are costed future plans, and since both education and schools are as complex as they are, the plans won't come easily.

The practicalities

Costing the plans: listing the costs

First ask, 'are *all* plans identified and listed?' At the start of LMS it was found ridiculously easy to overlook some items.

The major cost – staffing – is calculated by how many teacher periods of each subject are needed, systematically working through the projected curriculum. However, it is rather easier, for example, to overlook *services* you require, and have no intention of *doing without*, though they may not first come to mind. Typically, in the early days, the first wave of schools produced examples of 'forgetting' (or perhaps 'not realising') that of course they wanted dustbins emptied, cookers serviced, premises annually spring-cleaned in the holidays.

They also forgot that they planned (ie wanted) to retain depreciating assets. Five extra computers are always costed, but the fact that the replacement life of the 25 already in use means another five should be budgeted for might slip past. The tennis court surround-fence may not even need patching *this* year, but if it has a 15-year life span, and a cost of £30,000, you had better 'plan' somehow to 'reserve' £2,000 a year for its upkeep.

Furniture is a particular problem. Just what *is* the expected life span in this school of this quality of chair? A look at the throw-out rate (does the caretaker know it?) might provide a clue.

LMS itself is ensuring that a 'last year's list' of costings will be available, to prevent the overlooking of important costs. For schools new to delegated budgeting, a glance at the budgets of a couple of schools of similar size will be of immense help, though the percentage allocations to different headings may not be identical, either because of real cost differences (School A costs £10,000 more to heat to the same temperature than School B with the same Numbers on Roll (NOR)) or because of a difference in categorising (School A counts the caretaker as a non-teaching staff cost, School B counts him or her as a premises cost). However, more and more, as previous budgets become available, the annual cycle can focus mainly on changes.

So, the latter stage of budget creation, after plans are made, is the methodical writing down of lists of the implied activities/supplies/services, first making sure that the list is *complete*, and pondering over how the *annual* cost can be estimated/identified, and from what sources of information.

Pay and price changes

The price base constantly shifts: inflation happens; pay increases are awarded. It helps to choose an understood price base (eg the 'November price base' used by most LEAs) if you are using, as you will, a previous year's budget as a guide for the next. You can simply apply the current price plus an estimate for inflation during the year (but remember an estimated 10 per cent increase by the end of the year does not mean a 10 per cent increase for your budget, if some of it is spent before the end of the year). Most of this is methodical common sense, plus informed guesswork (eg on fuel prices), but the most important point about inflation is to remember that it happens, and to make allowances.

Quantity changes

Sensible use of last year's budget involves asking 'what is different' not just in price, but also in quantity. Because schools continually develop, so do the *proportions of activities* represented in the budget. A change in the curriculum may mean more science, less drama staffing (and of course, even though the cost in pounds may be the same, the personnel change needs careful management, to say the least!). These 'quantity' changes are most likely to relate to curriculum change, change in use or area of premises, and changes in NOR.

Focus on such changes enables us most easily to make use of previous budgets, by adjusting the quantities required for our future plans. Assuming we also retain an awareness of price changes, and put these into the sums, we can often stay on course. But not always. Sometimes after costing changes we find we are *disproportionately* better or worse off than before. This is because of fluctuations in income.

Income fluctuation

Income (the other starting point for budgets) is of course derived from the local LMS formula, which is largely, but not entirely, related to NOR. It is because costs are also largely, but not entirely, related that LMS budgets are possible – but when the two 'not entirelys' do not cancel each other out, there is a sudden deficit (or windfall).

This is *not* the perennial 'deficit' between anticipated income and desirable (but unfortunately unrealistic) expenditure. Part of the earlier process will be to gain a rough idea of how many of our desired plans can be afforded, and the plans will have been prioritised and modified (five new computers, not ten, four rooms redecorated, not eight, one teacher for that 'A' level Geography group of 22, not two, no satellite receiver dish, no bursar).

Often that prioritising is within categories which have strategic limits (eg there is an annual Information Technology (IT) expansion budget, so those five new computers beat the claims of other IT equipment, but could not trespass on the redecoration budget; there is a staffing number norm, such as a historic pupil-teacher ratio, so that Geography 'A' level demand for eight extra teacher periods was prioritised against the wish to split a large Year 10 science class – but not without debate on recosting strategic allocations against the school caretaking or cleaning or books budget). All that kind of adjustment goes on, much of it not even reaching the governing body, except as reports of final decisions or proposals within governor-agreed strategic norms.

However, a change in NOR may lead to a disproportionate loss or increase in LMS income (eg if a small-school allowance in the formula is gained or lost). More critically, school *costs* may not alter in line with NOR fluctuations. A few students more (or less) can alter dramatically the number of teachers required, as class size thresholds are passed. The loss of 40 sixth formers and 100K of income could reduce group size but leave *no* 'A' level group empty enough to collapse (real loss of spending power about 100K). Moreover, a school typically has 'fixed' premises costs (rates, heating, telephones, etc) and almost always will be *worse* off if NOR falls below capacity. When LEAs paid premises costs, this was a uniform tax on all schools; now it falls on the particular case.

So the same *budget* building process, based on the *same* curriculum, might 'work' one year and not the next. The moral is to know your local scheme well, to know its thresholds (and those of the school) and to plan and calculate *ahead*, because fluctuations, even if not changeable, might be spreadable over several years if foreseen (but are perhaps unmanageable if not).

The annual cycle

Finally, who works all this out, and when? Granted that everyone is in fact debating plans all the time, there must be decision-making moments when next year's plans are fixed, so that, from then, the continuing debate refers to following years. There must also be times for formal presentation to, discussion with, and approval by, governing bodies.

Typically, the governing body, though no doubt aware of and involved in ongoing ideas for development, will have a formal curriculum plan presented (often to a committee) in January/February, accompanied then or briefly afterwards by a staffing plan and a staffing number (at which time it can review its strategic norms for staffing). Any foreseen staffing problems (eg recruitment or redundancy) will need to be handled at once.

A draft budget, based on that curriculum and staffing, and on an assumed pay and prices increase, can be presented (again probably to a committee) around February (incorporating of course an estimate of LMS formula income). Any special projects or final priorities can be discussed. If approved, this budget framework can be refined and presented as a full budget in March/April, ready to send to the LEA (if a maintained school) in April/May.

CHECKLIST

1. Know your educational plans. They, and those who form them, form the budget.

2. Identify *all* plans for costing (including unspoken plans to maintain depreciating assets such as furniture, equipment, tennis courts, labs, office machinery).

3. Alert governing body if you want to propose adjustment to strategic norms.

4. Cost your plans – previous costs are a guide but:
   - Decide on a sensible level of reserves (5%?) and try to build that in.
   - Remember to adjust for *price changes* from last year to date, and from now to the following year-end. It helps to show pay and price assumptions separately.
   - Remember to adjust for *quantity changes*, trying to keep cost/ changes in line with NOR. This is difficult, though you can try applying NOR to such items as departmental capitation, or minutes of support time, etc, per pupil.
   - Cost each staff member individually, not forgetting increments, allowances, on-costs, pay increases (often staged).

5. Identify any disproportionate rises/falls in costs (eg class-size thresholds passed, causing larger than pro-rata additions/reductions in staffing on the current curriculum).

6. Apply NOR to current local LMS formula to produce 'income'. Check for any formula changes or thresholds crossed (eg small-school allowance gained or lost). Check if LMS budget (corrected for inflation) is up or down in line with NOR.

7. Match 4 to 6. Alert everyone if the costs/income match is different from last year and make plans to deal with windfalls/deficits not arising out of *your* educational planning.

8. Formally present, discuss; if necessary modify, gain approval.

9. Start planning for next year and the year after.

The Finance Function in Grant-maintained Schools

John Chastney and Howard Jackson

Before a school becomes grant-maintained (GM), the governors, head and senior management team will have to make many decisions which will have a major bearing on the efficient and effective running of the school. The introduction of Local Management of Schools (LMS) schemes will have helped schools prepare for some of the impact of GM status. The first GM schools have been operating since September 1989 and valuable information has been built up since then.

Accounting systems

A school can provide an accounting system, ranging from manual operation to a very powerful computer accounts package. It is vital that it can provide the information required by the Department for Education (DFE), the governing body, various sub-committees, the senior management team and all budget holders.

Manual accounts are very time-consuming, especially when extracting relevant financial information. In order to be able to produce the information required, a cash book, purchase day book, purchase ledger, sales ledger and nominal ledger will all be essential. A manual system will cost little to install and operate, and keeping manual accounts could be a good method for learning about accounting principles in preparation for future computerisation. This is particularly important for those new to the finance function.

Producing reports manually, however, often takes a considerable amount of time.

Software packages vary in quality and price. There are now several designed specifically for GM schools, and some provide flexible training on a one-to-one basis at the school.

Accounting principles

Schools account on a cash basis: the amount they record as spent is equal to the amount they have paid out. GM schools have to account on the basis of accruals accounting. This matches the expense shown in the accounts with the expense actually incurred during that period, irrespective of the amount paid out. For example, under the cash basis, if electricity is paid quarterly in arrears, commencing in April, there will be no charge for electricity in the accounts for the first quarter (end of June), because no invoice will have been received from the electricity distribution company. Accruals accounting makes an adjustment in the accounts to allow for this, and an estimate of the cost of electricity consumed would be included in the first quarter's accounts. The expense has been incurred and, therefore, it should be shown in the accounts.

Conversely, prepayments (payments made in advance of receiving the service, eg insurance, examination fees, telephone rentals, contract agreements) would be allowed.

Bursar's role

The role of the bursar is perceived differently from school to school.

Using the existing secretarial staff for the finance function may save costs but the saving may not be as great as envisaged. There may be other latent or apparent costs such as the need to engage external auditors to complete the accounts at year end. Some schools favour appointing finance staff at this level because it leaves the teachers in full control of the school.

At the other extreme, a specialist financial manager can operate the whole financial administration. He or she should have the ability to report to the interested parties as appropriate; be able to monitor expenditure accurately and produce the necessary budgets to enable the management of the school to function properly; have the ability to negotiate contracts for the benefit of the school; be able to manage the non-academic side of the school in a way that supports the school's aims and objectives. This may be achieved through the letting of part of the building, the use of surplus funds and investment policy, and other entrepreneurial methods. The bursar may also have responsibility for the buildings to ensure that they both meet the needs of the school, and that the necessary health, safety and insurance requirements are fulfilled.

The school must ensure that the complement of finance staff is adequate to support the school's activities. It is vital to remember also that the accounting function is there to help, support and guide people. It is not there to rule the school. The finance function requires an ability to understand the past, the present and the future, not just in short-term planning but also in a longer-term strategy within the school's development plan.

The budget process

The annual budget should be agreed well in advance of the financial year to which it applies: in most GM schools this will be around January of each year, when schools are notified by the Department for Education (DFE) of their notional Annual Maintenance Grant allocations for the financial year commencing in April.

Governors should be involved in some part of the process of producing the budget and should obtain final approval. Many schools invite departmental heads to bid for funds, while others issue definitive statements on allocations for the coming year.

We recommend that the bursar, headteacher and senior management team produce the draft budget with sub-committees of governors reviewing relevant aspects. The whole budget would then feed into the finance sub-committee for ratification, then to the full governing body for approval. At this stage, the bursar will produce income and expenditure estimates and cashflow estimates profiled into individual months of the financial year. These profiles are submitted to the DFE and, if the DFE is satisfied, a grant will be paid in accordance to the cashflow profile.

Commitment accounting

Commitment accounting is the method of recording the proposed expenditure of a budget. If a budget holder receives a budget of £5,000 for a year and commits him or herself to spending, say, £1,000 each term on teaching materials, he or she has £2,000 available to spend on other items. Commitment accounting shows not only the amount spent but also the amount committed for the

rest of the financial year. All GM schools should be capable of producing this information.

The headteacher as a businessperson

In many ways, running a GM school is like running a business and many of the basic principles for success or failure in financial terms are similar: a GM school needs both a good leader and a good manager as its head. Governors of GM schools have very great powers and responsibilities and are responsible for the school. But it is the head and SMT who make things happen.

It is of tremendous assistance to have an accountant on the governing body, especially during the transitional period when new financial systems, which will enable the school to meet the new demands placed on it, are designed and implemented.

Negotiation contracts

Obtaining GM status may allow schools to enter into new contracts or provide an opportunity to renegotiate contracts already in existence. Contracts may cover:

- school meals
- other catering services
- building maintenance – architects
                       – surveyors
- cleaning services
- grounds maintenance
- accountancy and audit
- computers – hardware
            – software
- personnel services
- banking
- insurance
- payroll

It is vital to obtain several tenders and, even more important, to dispose of the old maxim, 'cheapest is best'. Contracts accepted should represent the best value for money and should best meet the needs of the school. When looking at tenders, examine the way the service will be delivered, who will carry out the work, the price, the settlement terms, commitments on price increases, let-out clauses and break clauses.

Payroll

It is important to ensure that all staff are paid correctly and at the right time. Many options to administer payroll are available:

- existing local education authority (LEA)
- an LEA other than that previously responsible for the school
- a bureau (eg bank or accountants)
- self supply by the school.

The service should include producing all the relevant details and administering actual salary payments through an automated credit system (eg BACS), completing payments to the Inland Revenue, TPA (superannuation), production of payslips, completion of year-end returns at a set price.

Schools should be cautious about preparing their own payrolls, not because it is intrinsically difficult but because it is inherently dangerous. It may not be cheaper than buying in the service if the time of the finance staff is taken into consideration. Payroll is being run effectively in a number of GM schools where they benefit from employing people skilled in the process. Certain payroll information must be easily accessible to ensure compliance with ever-changing legislation and regulations. The system must also enable the school to monitor the budget effectively.

Some schools have combined their personnel services with payroll production. This may be helpful but is not essential.

Auditors

The school's auditors will perform a first-term survey to meet the requirements of the DFE. This can be performed in one of two ways: the auditors can be guided completely by the DFE and its format for the first-term survey, or they can offer an enhanced service which looks at various methods, systems and controls within the school. A management letter from the auditors will detail serious weaknesses and should suggest remedial methods. This letter should be seen as constructive and supportive.

The advice of auditors can extend into taxation, especially VAT, the budget process, contract negotiation and personnel and company law.

Financial manual

Each school must produce its own financial manual as soon as possible, preferably within its first term of incorporation. The manual should be very much a working document and not something produced to satisfy the DFE. It should be used as a reference document for the relevant personnel and should be kept secure. It will enable the school to continue operating should something unforeseen happen to the finance personnel.

The audit team will use the manual to understand how the school operates and who is involved. The manual should include an organisational chart showing the lines of responsibility and also detailed descriptions of the roles played by each individual on the chart, accounting systems and controls operated within the school, documentation and records kept by the school, security of records and equipment, the budgeting process, reporting timetable and format of reports, financial decisions of the governing body and various sub-committees, details of the computerised systems, lists of all the external advisers and contractors with contact names and telephone numbers.

Recently the Audit Commission has expressed more than a little interest in GM schools. If the Commission investigates the GM sector, we are confident that it will wish to see up-to-date financial manuals in all schools and find evidence that the systems operate as recorded and are adequate for the school's needs.

Segregation of duties

Regulations are quite clear when it comes to segregation of duties: applying those regulations in a way that is workable can sometimes be extremely difficult, especially in the small schools with fewer staff among whom to allocate the duties. It is necessary to ensure that one person alone cannot complete a full transaction, from ordering goods to paying for them and all the elements between.

The finance sub-committee should ensure that safeguards are built into the system and should regularly monitor the financial affairs of the school. It should also, as and when required, receive reports including income and expenditure budgets, cashflow projections, income and expenditure against budget, variance reports and monthly management accounts.

Capital bids

Once a year, schools are invited to bid for a capital allocation to enable them either to extend or improve their facilities. The criteria for applying for a capital grant is clearly laid down by the DFE but the quality of the bids differ tremendously from school to school. Professional help should be sought when putting the bid together from architects or other building professionals who possess both the experience and expertise to deal with a large government department, preferably in the education sector. Unfortunately, if a school's capital bid is rejected, there is no additional funding available to pay the professional fees incurred in the submission.

Supplementary to capital bids, each school currently receives a formula allocation based on its number of pupils. This has to be applied for in accordance with set criteria and enables schools to do minor capital works, but cannot be used to bolster the building maintenance budget.

VAT and tax

All GM schools have to pay VAT and, at present, receive a grant based on 2.5 per cent of the Annual Maintenance Grant (AMG), less mandatory rate relief, ie 80 per cent of rates.

On incorporation, GM schools bcome charities by statute and, for this reason, receive mandatory 80 per cent rate relief. Although GM schools may be disadvantaged by VAT, overall, they will gain by receiving interest gross from bank accounts or investments.

Caution is required when approaching the threshold for VAT registration (in 1993–94 this is £37,600 of turnover). Turnover may include catering, lettings, school shop or tuck shop. But there could also be potential problems with school trips abroad, drama productions, field studies, sports activities and orchestral visits overseas. If in doubt, it is advisable to speak to accountants who employ their own tax experts to guide and advise: they will also be able to advise on other areas of concern such as tax on covenants and avoidance of corporation tax.

Annual maintenance grant (AMG)

Annual maintenance grant is presently based on the school's local authority LMS scheme and is made up of three elements:

1. direct costs as determined by LMS scheme;

2. central costs, currently 15 per cent of LMS but depends on number of GM schools within a particular authority;

3. school meals subsidy based on the meals subsidy used by the local authority multiplied by the number of pupils from Form 7 the previous financial year (both paid and free meals).

The AMG is usually paid in 12 equal installments with perhaps an initial payment on the day of incorporation or on 1 April in subsequent years, which is deducted from the final installment in the following March. AMG payments are usually made approximately three days before the date the school pays its staff and are credited direct to the school's nominated bank account.

Transitional grant

A transitional grant is given to schools to enable them to prepare for GM status. The future of the transitional grant is in doubt because many schools have undertaken major developments under LMS. Many schools already have the necessary hardware and software, personnel and offices to meet the growing demands of greater delegation.

Meeting deadlines from the DFE and various committees

The DFE experts information monthly, quarterly and annually in the format of the GMS forms. Form GMS3, income and expenditure budget, and form GMS4, cashflow projections, have to be submitted in January on notification of the school's AMG for the following financial year. Other forms are: GMS5, monthly cash statement; form GMS6, quarterly income and expenditure account and projected outturn figures for the whole of the financial year; and form GMS8, year-end accounts including governor's report, auditor's report, income and expenditure accounts, statement of financial position, balance sheet, cashflow statement, notes to the accounts and finally a detailed income and expenditure account. Annual returns on form GMS9 and form SPG(D), special purpose grant development proposals, all have to be submitted in January each year for the following year. Form GMS10 is required before the end of August, reporting on actual expenditure on form SPG(D) for the previous financial year. Internal committees need to be supplied with information before they meet.

What happens if things go wrong?

No school can have a cumulative deficit. Schools should not expect the DFE to assist them financially should they get into financial difficulties, but the DFE would expect a detailed report from the school showing how and by when it proposes to resolve the situation.

Depending on the scale of the problem, the school may be required to instigate drastic measures to rectify its financial position. This may include the cancellation of all building improvements, restricting purchase of any additional equipment or educational consumables, desperate measures to reduce all overhead costs and, possibly, a reduction of staffing costs.

Most of the problems arise through mismanagement. With autonomy comes many additional responsibilities and worries, but also the freedom, when managed well, to make the decisions that will greatly benefit the individual school.

3.3

Introducing Accounting and Computer Systems into Grant-maintained Schools

John Davies

Obtaining grant-maintained status means a fundamental change in management responsibility by the headteachers and governors. The school now has to operate financially like a commercial enterprise.

Why are some businesses successful and others not? In most cases it is due to management's failure to understand in good time what is going on and to take the necessary corrective action. This is often due to inadequate accounting structures, or the lack of trained financial and accounting staff with an ability to read the figures, control the business and take remedial action.

Schools are not very different from small- to medium-size firms and need similar financial and management structures. Some managers, and no doubt some headteachers, think all that is required is someone to keep the books to pay wages and bills, and that anything beyond that is an unnecessary overhead. Firms who act like that do not survive.

If management is to have tight control it has to have systems to record and measure what is happening, in order to plan and compare against budget what is happening, in order to plan and compare against budget and take management decisions to improve efficiency, cut costs and obtain value for money.

Independent schools have always been in this situation, but in recent years, with the rapidly rising cost of education often outstripping inflation, they have had to improve their accounting structures and with it the calibre of the financial staff.

Grant-maintained schools have to operate in the same way to be successful as educational bodies and financially efficient. The Department for Education's Financial Controls, Reporting, Auditing and Systems Accounting Requirements certainly demand this.

Staffing

Grant-maintained school headteachers need to have a good accountant/bursar, just as they have to have a good deputy for the academic side. The headteacher should acquire some financial training so that he or she can understand what the bursar is presenting in the financial accounts and management reports.

The bursar has to be capable of producing accounts up to income and expenditure and balance sheet level, as well as management reports such as budgets, forecasts and cash flow statements. He or she must be able to structure the accounts so the financial information is easily digestible for governors, headteachers and heads of departments in order that they can take effective management decisions.

It is essential that the bursar is computer literate; it is inconceivable in this day and age to run an efficient accounting system without the aid of good applications systems software. He or she should have a thorough understanding of how the system works and be able to maximise the benefits of the facilities available. The availability now of powerful desk-top personal computers at reasonable prices makes it possible to install quite large systems for accounting and other related purposes.

The accounting system

The minimum accounting system a school should contemplate is a nominal ledger to accommodate all the income and expenditure accounts for both revenue and capital items. The subsidiary ledgers which provide other information for the nominal ledger are the payroll and the purchase ledger. As the school is financed by per capita grants, there would not normally be a need for a fees ledger as in independent schools, unless it was intended to provide such things as extra subjects not covered by the grant. However, it would be beneficial to set up either a fees or a sales ledger to deal with income from non-grant sources and to be able to integrate it with the rest of the system. It is important to take great care in structuring the nominal accounts in a logical way to reflect the various areas of revenue and capital expenditure, particularly for summarising and presentation into the financial accounts and management reports.

As it is assumed the accountancy function will be computerised, it is suggested that a five-digit number be used for each nominal account. The first two digits would designate the major sectors of revenue or capital expenditure and the last three, the subsections. This would allow for a logical structure to subgroup areas of expenditure and could be easily expanded for future needs. Being numeric only, it is also quicker for inputting information using the right-hand number keys on the keyboard. The application software bought for the nominal ledger should have facilities to set up management reports in the style required by the school and to have the ability to accept budget figures and obtain variance reports. It should be capable of obtaining all the detailed information needed either as hard copy or on the screen, whether current or historical. The double entry should be checked automatically so the trial balance is always in balance.

The nominal ledger should be able to accept automatically, by interfacing, the information from the subsidiary ledgers.

The purchase ledger should have the ability to post invoices, credit notes and payments to suppliers' ledger accounts or as one-off transactions. It should have the facility to pay accounts automatically on the due date pre-set in the ledger, either by computer-printed cheques or direct to the supplier's bank account via the modem and the Bankers Automatic Clearing Service (BACS). The latter method makes the bank reconciliation much easier as there is only one payment for all suppliers paid on a particular date rather than checking all the unpresented cheques. Cost centre reports, cash flow and a full history of all transactions should be available as well as creditor listings and supplier ledger accounts for management control. Another essential is a purchase ordering system that is linked to the purchase ledger, a very useful integration of checks and controls. This way orders can be printed and the total commitment monitored as a check on departmental spending at any time and the future cash flow kept under review.

A good payroll package is obviously important as any errors in pay soon cause consternation among the staff. Anyone who has run a payroll system knows the time taken in sorting out employees' pay queries, imagined or real. There is a need to input this information in great detail so all the various management reports can be extracted as required.

Payroll systems need to be able to deal with income tax, national insurance, Statutory Sick Pay (SSP), Statutory Maternity Pay (SMP), pensions and other deductions. Employee pay constitutes the major portion of a school's costs. On top of the basic salary there is anything up to an extra one-third, for the employer's contributions to pensions, national insurance and the cost of holidays and sickness. Therefore this expenditure needs monitoring very carefully. As with the purchase ledger, it is beneficial if the pay can be given on computer-produced cheques; better still, payment direct to the bank or building society by BACS. Another essential in the software is that it will produce the year-end tax and national insurance returns for the Inland Revenue together with the annual pensions returns.

Historical payroll information is extremely useful in structuring the salary and wage cost area of the budget. The foregoing has summarised what is needed in a practical accounting system for schools to ensure they have the control and flexibility not only to keep the obligatory records but also for the school to measure the results of its decisions and monitor efficiency.

Computer systems

When looking at the different systems offered by various companies, investigate what they can provide outside the core accounting package. Firms that have specialised on schools are more likely to be sympathetic to the educational environment and can probably offer software that is complementary to the financial side.

Spreadsheets, word processing, databases, asset registers, school shop, estate management, library, appeals and donations and desktop publishing software are systems that may need to be considered for the future. If they are all available from the same supplier this will reduce the operational headaches and probably the overall cost as well. When there is a problem and there are a number of different suppliers, it is difficult to know where to place the responsibility. This can be frustrating both for the user waiting for the problem to be dealt with and for the support staff who are unable to continue with their work.

When planning the structure of the computer system, the compatibility of the various packages should not be overlooked.

Worth mentioning, but not directly connected with the financial side, is the availability of a good schools administration package for academic reports, pupil attendance, curriculum and examination planning and timetabling; and perhaps a separate accounting system to exploit the school's assets to generate additional income from non-academic sources.

Security of the system is essential so that no unauthorised

personnel can access it. The software packages should be protected by passwords at various levels so users can only work on the programme allocated to them. If the computer is on-line by modem it should be switched off when not in use. Likewise, if the processor is provided with a mechanical lock it should be secured when the system is shut down. It is very wise to take a back up copy at least daily of updated data, more often if there has been an especially large input that would be difficult to recreate.

Devices to smooth power fluctuations which can give rise to problems can be fitted for a reasonable cost, more expensive is equipment that allows time to close the system down in a power cut.

This gives a brief idea of what to look for in schools accounting and administration computer systems. The very detailed instructions and the information contained in the DFE Rainbow package gives a comprehensive check on what the systems should be able to offer.

Choosing a software supplier

When choosing a software house it has already been recommended to look at firms that have tended to specialise in the educational field. Fortunately, the independent sector has been an area which has created a demand over the last decade. In this period a lot of specialist programmes have been developed. These companies should now have adapted their applications software to the needs of the grant-maintained schools, particularly in the areas for producing the DFE requirements such as the Grant-maintained Account and Report Forms.

Things to be examined when choosing a supplier area are the quality and sophistication of the software and the back up given in terms of training in-house and on-site and support by telephone and modem. Make sure that the company has been in business for a reasonable length of time, is big enough to carry a sizeable professional staff, has a large client base and is financially sound. See if the company's clients have user groups to whom you can talk. Many small companies depend on a few key staff and if they leave, or the firm collapses or is taken over, the school can be left in a very difficult situation.

It is advisable to take out maintenance contracts on both software application programmes and hardware equipment then, if things go wrong as they occasionally do, the systems can be back on-line as soon as possible. Software problems should be solved quickly by telephone or modem by the supplier. In the case of hardware, you need an engineer on call to rectify equipment faults, so choose a company who carry essential spares in stock and have good repair facilities. Non-contract clients cannot expect the same priority and speed of response and in the long term it might cost more. At least contract costs can be budgeted for.

The auditors should be involved, especially in the early stages, to check that the audit trails are to their satisfaction.

To give the bursar support in the early stages it would be advisable to employ a consultant who can help design and implement the systems and give back up and training to the staff until everything is up and running satisfactorily. The amount of extra work required until software and hardware is installed and proved should not be underestimated. If no support is forthcoming in the beginning, the whole system may be badly conceived, designed and implemented which would be very difficult and costly to rectify at a later date.

3.4

Insurance

David Nichols

Insurance is a complex subject which merits careful scrutiny. It is one of those areas where schools which remain under Local Education Authority (LEA) control have the clear advantage of specialist staff to advise them and to negotiate on their behalf.

Each LEA has considerable, if lessening, discretion as to the degree to which responsibility for insurance is retained or delegated to schools. In practice, LEAs are usually very keen and able to provide support and advice to the schools which they maintain. The recent problems with Municipal Mutual Insurance have, however, shown that such advice is not infallible.

Schools which are not maintained by an LEA obviously do not have the opportunity to participate in these centrally negotiated arrangements and must arrange their own cover in all the areas discussed in this chapter.

When first considering insurance the following steps should be taken:

1. Governors and budget managers of LEA-maintained schools should make contact with the LEA's Insurance Department to ascertain exactly which elements of insurance are covered by centrally negotiated and funded policies and which are left to the discretion of individual schools.

2. Two lists should then be drawn up: one noting all forms of insurance which are provided automatically by the LEA and the second detailing all forms of risk for which the school is itself responsible.

3. Advice should be sought as to whether the LEA has negotiated

any group purchase arrangements for those aspects of insurance which have been delegated to schools. Such arrangements can usually offer considerable savings on premiums when compared with individually negotiated packages. It is, however, always worth obtaining independent quotes from reputable insurers to provide a comparison.

4. Advice should be sought as to which insurance companies offer the most suitable packages where no centrally negotiated policy exists.

What to insure

The major areas requiring insurance fall into the following categories.

Buildings and contents

Generally, the LEA insures centrally for structural damage and repairs, leaving the smaller items, such as glazing, plumbing, interior and exterior and decoration and minor roof repairs to the individual school. The LEA retains responsibility for any large machinery or plant on school premises.

The exact division between that for which the school is responsible and that for which the LEA is responsible varies considerably. It is important therefore that governors and budget managers are absolutely clear as to the extent of their liability. Most LEAs publish a document setting out exactly where responsibility lies for all aspects of building maintenance from curtain tracks to filtration systems for swimming pools.

Schools which derive a high income from public lettings should also ascertain whether they are insured through the LEA for consequential loss should buildings be rendered unusable for a prolonged period.

All fixtures, fittings and contents are the school's responsibility and it is normal to arrange an 'All Perils' policy to cover buildings and contents. This is likely to be the most expensive essential insurance item delegated to a school and many LEAs have negotiated their own reduced premium schemes which can offer good value.

There are also policies available to cover any specific, high-cost items, such as computers and audio-visual equipment, which may be excluded from the general policy. It is important for the budget manager to be aware of exactly what any policy does cover and to consider whether it is worth insuring those items which are excluded.

One aspect to check is the extent, if any, to which the personal belongings of staff, governors and visitors are covered on school premises.

Most buildings and contents policies carry an excess, the level of which may influence a decision on insuring individual items.

Public and employer's liability

It is normal practice for LEAs to take out a central policy to cover both employer's liability and public liability. Governing bodies need to ascertain that they are covered by such a policy and, if not, to effect cover immediately.

These policies will generally include cover for such risks as professional negligence, slander and libel. The delegated powers now possessed by governors and headteachers increase the possibility of them being subject to civil action, so this is a priority area.

A recent EC draft directive on the liability of suppliers of services, if ratified, could have serious implications, particularly in relation to injuries received as a result of school sporting activities. Governors should ensure that they have up-to-date information on this matter.

Fidelity guarantee

Here again the LEA is likely to insure all its staff centrally against fraud or 'infidelity'. The governors need to ensure that they are also covered by this policy. It is also a good idea to examine whether it has been, or could be, extended to cover non-public funds and the PTA.

Legal costs

As the employer, the LEA takes responsibility for the legal costs involved in defending actions for unfair dismissal and for issues concerning employment legislation.

An individual school will not normally need to purchase insurance for these purposes, although governors should check with their LEA that they are covered for actions against them concerning the operation of pay and promotion policies within the school.

In non-LEA schools, where the governors are the employers, insurance must be arranged in the same manner as any private company.

Personal accident

While this form of insurance is usually provided by the LEA, the extent and detail varies considerably. It is therefore worthwhile examining exactly what has been provided and considering whether the governing body wishes to augment this cover.

The four main categories to check are:

1. Staff, teaching and non-teaching, within school, on extra-curricular and off-site activites and travelling to and from school;

2. governors on school duties;

3. visitors and volunteer workers within school;

4. pupils within school, on extra-curricular and off-site activities and on work-experience placements.

It is worth noting that some schools are encouraging parents to insure their own children.

PTA and public access events

Under Local Management of Schools (LMS) schools are moving more and more towards generating their own income. When large events are held involving public access and/or the handling of large amounts of cash, the need for insurance is self-evident.

PTAs have traditionally arranged their own insurance, but this may now be unnecessary as many LEA organised policies already applied to schools include such fund-raising events in their schedules as normal school activities. This certainly merits investigation by governors and the PTA as it could lead to savings.

School visits

While LEAs will mostly be found to cover all their staff against accidents and other problems incurred whilst exercising their professional duties in or out of school, this is not normally the case with pupils. The only exception to this being if the accident or injury occurs as a result of negligence by the school or its staff.

It is therefore important that, when planning trips over any considerable distance or period, schools should check on what type of cover is necessary and what is available. There are many options and, while travel companies will usually offer a competitive all-in package, it is essential to examine the small print, check on any excess payable and seek alternative quotes for comparison. The principal categories to check for cover are:

1. Personal, accident/illness;

2. loss of, or damage to, belongings;

3. vehicles owned by the party, including provision for breakdown.

It is especially important, when planning visits to privately run outdoor activity centres, to ensure that all the staff employed by the centre, who will have responsibility for children's safety, are appropriately qualified and that comprehensive personal accident policies are in place.

Contractors

Schools should ensure that any contractor employed upon their premises has a suitable public liability insurance policy. As a rough guideline, such a policy should allow for a minimum of £2 million cover where major works are concerned and £1 million for all minor works.

In practice most reputable contractors do carry this kind of policy, but it is in the school's interest to ensure that this is so in all cases.

Cover for absent staff

An interesting one! In the heady early days of LMS, brokers and insurance companies were keen to get in on the act, often offering very low premiums. Fingers were burned and the approach is now more sober, with higher premiums. Indeed, some schools may experience difficulty in organising cover for this risk.

Many LEAs have negotiated a central package with an insurance company for funding supply teachers to cover for absent staff for a fixed period of time, eg from the third to twentieth day of absence. The details vary, as does the amount paid out per day of cover. The premiums are usually calculated on a set figure per member of staff on the school's establishment. There are also independently operated schemes which may be worth consideration.

Some schools have chosen to gamble on a healthy staff and placed a sum equivalent to the insurance premium into a contingency fund for supply cover in the hope that much of it will not be used. This clearly is the sort of gamble which insurance seeks to avoid, but a school which gambles luckily can save a fair amount. For example, 58 members of staff at an annual premium of £160 adds up to £9,280. Clearly this is an issue which many governing bodies will want to discuss.

Forward planning

When the school is clear as to the extent of its own needs, care needs to be taken to establish when policies become operative and when they are renewable. It should also be clear when premiums will be payable and exactly how much is involved in each policy, as the budget manager will need to calculate a total projected insurance budget well before 1 April each year in order to set an accurate budget.

3.5

The Finance Office and the Role of the Bursar

Maureen Cruickshank

Changing roles

Headteachers, their deputies and other senior managers in schools rarely acknowledge the success of (LMS), and yet equally rarely do they express any wish to turn the clock back and give up the recently acquired ownership of their budgets. This is understandable, since enjoyment of their new autonomy is often marred by the difficulties of managing with resources that appear more tightly constrained year by year. But just how much time should heads, deputies and any other teaching staff spend poring over the minutiae of budgets and balance sheets? Senior managers should decide policies and priorities, but the implementation of the budget should be left to the finance office and the bursar. LMS has enhanced the role played by financial staff in maintained schools – they are gradually gaining a similar status to that of their colleagues in independent schools.

All school managers should think creatively about the match of people to tasks. A golden rule should be that no teachers do any tasks which could be done more economically and possibly more efficiently by administrative staff.

Peter Mortimore and his team did some interesting research on innovative uses of non-teaching staff which was published in 1992. Several of the case studies looked at innovation concerning the role of the bursar[1].

Fortunately, in most cases the finance office has coped very well with the necessity to acquire new skills and competencies to operate SIMS and other systems. Sometimes it has been possible for schools to make a new or additional appointment to the role of bursar (sometimes called registrar or administrator). School managers need to think carefully about the job description for this role.

Should the bursar also act as clerk to the governors?

This is common practice in independent schools. LEA officers are excellent clerks, but governors and school managers will be quick to appreciate the greater accessibility of a clerk who works within the school, particularly for example in the labyrinth of regulations and arrangements for exclusion of pupils, and of course there is a financial saving on the charges levied by the LEA for providing clerking.

Should the bursar be a member of the senior management team?

Practice varies. Some bursars do not attend meetings of senior managers, some have partial membership and others have full membership. The most important factor is that nobody feels he or she is wasting time. It is often refreshing to have the view of a lay person when curricular issues are being discussed.

Generation of income

Quite frequently a bursar's job description will contain a paragraph about generating additional funds/resources from parents, local communities, government agencies and industry. It may also refer to oversight of school bookings and lettings to ensure maximum effective use of buildings and facilities.

Premises responsibilities

A good bursar will lighten the load on heads, deputies and senior managers with regard to premises and buildings and free their time for duties more closely related to the curriculum. Very many schools have managed to find funds within their budgets for minor building improvements or even projects for extensions and new buildings. A bursar with good administrative skills can take on tasks such as commissioning architects, going out to tender, arranging site meetings, liaising with contractors and, finally, making arrangements for the official opening of the new premises. In periods of recession, schools have been able to engage in building work at around 25 per cent less cost than before the recession, with builders putting in low tenders in order to obtain contracts and maintain their workforce.

Cleaning and catering contracts

When a school decides not to renew a contract with LEA cleaners and school meals, a bursar can deal with the specifications, advertisements, placing of contracts and monitoring of new arrangements. It may be possible to effect some savings and to tailor the specification more precisely to the needs of the school.

The finance office

Depending on circumstances, some schools are taking the option of using the extended cheque book scheme while others are remaining with the County Hall central payments scheme. Whichever scheme is chosen, LMS has inevitably increased the workload of the finance office. To meet this increase, a critical look must be taken at the organisation of the office. Every member must have clearly defined responsibilities and the office must have a set routine. Financial reporting deadlines have to be met, but more importantly, accounts should be paid on time to take advantage of any discounts. It is also an advantage if the finance office can be located separately from the main office with fewer distractions. Initially set routines and timings for the office may seem bureaucratic to other members of staff, but they do pay dividends.

Budget and review timetable

A good bursar will cajole senior mangement into a timetable of forward planning which could consist of five stages:

- Stage 1 – review (by end of September)
- Stage 2 – policy and priorities (by end of October)
- Stage 3 – proposal for next financial year (by end of November)
- Stage 4 – next year's budget (by end of January)
- Stage 5 – agreement of next year's budget by the governors (by end of February)

Alongside the forward planning, the bursar will of course be providing regular budget updates for the current financial year by senior management and for the governors' finance sub-committee.

Recruitment of the bursar

Advertisements generally result in large numbers of applications from a wide variety of sources. There are several instances of 'poacher turning gamekeeper' when staff working centrally with the LEA apply for posts in schools. It is then fascinating to observe the switch of these loyalties from the corporate identity to the interests of the single institution.

Such staff bring with them good contacts, often excellent training in administrative and financial procedures, and knowledge of computing systems.

The armed services frequently encourage officers who are retiring to apply to be bursars in independent schools. Recently there has been a growth in applications from service personnel to vacancies in the state sector, resulting in many successful appointments.

The recession has also brought benefits to school staffing, not just in better qualified entrants to teaching, but also to all administrative posts in schools, including the bursar and other financial staff. The difficulties faced by new graduates when seeking employment are making many of them consider almost any non-teaching vacancy which is advertised by a school.

Salary of the bursar

Post-LMS, the tendency was for schools to offer a higher salary than LEAs had previously, particularly because of the additional responsibilities of the post after LMS and partly because LEAs had tended to create better career prospects in central administration than in schools. The recession may have halted this trend. As we come out of recession it is likely that the upward trend will resume, taking the state school bursar's salary closer to that paid by the independent sector.

References

1   Mortimore P, Mortimore J with Hywel Thomas and Rosemary Cairns, Brenda Taggart *The innovative uses of non-teaching staff in primary and secondary schools Project*, Institute of Education, University of London, October, 1992.

Part Four

Human Resource Management

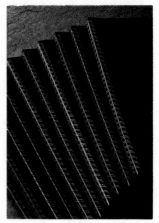

Working with Governors

Joan Sallis

Why we have to get it right

The legislation of the 1980s and 1990s has left schools very exposed. Exposed by the 1988 Act to the cold winds of the market place: cold winds released by testing and league tables, formula funding with its pressure to survive and to recruit, and competition from new kinds of publicly funded schools. Exposed also by the 1992 Act to regular inspection and published reports, and take-over by hit squads if schools are judged to be failing. Exposed by the 1993 Act possibly to new masters, operating by as yet undefined principles, with power to reshape the system. Compelled by all three Acts to be more open and more accountable. There are no everlasting arms underneath those who fall.

All the new responsibilities of schools, *and* the dangers they face, are shared under these Acts with a group of people who are not educators, but who have voluntarily undertaken the support and supervision of schools. This in itself constitutes a new and daunting task for some heads. But failure to build the partnership and make it real puts schools at even greater risk, for only common purpose and trust can survive in these strong seas. It is a professional challenge like no other. Here are some practical guidelines to help in building the partnership.

The new-style governors, and tomorrow's head teachers

We have moved on from seats in the front row, and mutters of 'Well, I'm sure we can safely leave this to the headmaster' (even if it was a

headmistress). Some day soon a headteacher will regard an open and mutually respectful working relationship with governors as a task worthy of professional pride, the finest flowering of management talent.

First, however, may I surprise you by addressing my first words to deputy heads as they wait in the wings? It may be unbelievable, but there are thousands of schools to my knowledge – from my postbag, governor training sessions and face-to-face encounters – where deputy heads will never have any swimming lessons in that deep water of the world outside the staffroom, the world of the law and regulations, the Local Education Authority (LEA), the political parties, pressure groups, and above all governors, until they land with a bellyflop. They tell me, six months later, that they almost drowned.

Not just cheap but free

The in-service training that is not just cheap, but free, is top-priority preparation for tomorrow's heads. Some LEAs neglect it too, but that is no reason why the school should not ensure that deputies at least know their governors, come to meetings, share in preparing the head's report, and have some practice in making school issues come alive for non-educationists.

The headteachers who will be moving to one side in the next decade will either be the older ones or the not-so-old ones who haven't liked the way schools have changed. In choosing their successors, governors will be looking above all for faces upturned to the future, governor-friendly faces, faces reflecting minds already focused on the task of managing schools in a new collaborative way.

You can't blame them, for it has been irritating to turn from all the hype about partnership in the training guides, the newspapers, and the speeches of politicians, to the pretences of many real situations, the desperate plea for new white lines to keep governors out or, at the other extreme, the rhetoric about sharing from those who have not yet realised how much sharing hurts.

Professional pride is a powerful engine, and if we could only attach it to the task of making participatory structures as much an object of such pride as the teaching in the classroom, then we should really be on the move. Often, however, the structures of governance are seen as something external to the real job of managing schools, and headteachers who would be ashamed to say their staff were awful because it would reflect on their leadership skills, are not embarrassed to say this about governors. This is a service devoted to the development of human beings, yet one set of human beings is seen as unsuitable for development.

Starting points

'My governors are so supportive'	— (the drunk and the lamp-post support welcome, illumination less so)
'I'm quite lucky really, my governors don't bother me all that often'	— (the Victorian wife thinks of England)
'They mean well but they are out of their depth'	— (I didn't choose them, why should I be proud or ashamed?)
'I wouldn't submit to surgery by a hospital porter'	— (Why must the teacher alone be plagued by interfering amateurs?)

Table 4.1.1 *Some give-away lines*

Attitudes must change, however, before ways can be changed. This new dimension of school management must be seen as inevitable, legitimate and, above all, necessary if public education is to have powerful friends again in a hostile world. The perspective of lay people must be respected as valid and complementary: the purpose is to use it, not change it into a poor imitation of an educator's perspective. There must be the will to share *even when the powers to be shared increase*. It's easy to be benevolent with what you haven't got. Take the two Welsh farmers who were discussing communism:

> 'Oh I know it's out-of-fashion, but I really do believe in it. Share and share alike, innit? If I had two 'ouses, I'd give you one Dai, and if I had two cars I'd give you one.'
> *'What if you had two pigs?'*
> 'Oh that's different innit? I got two pigs.'

The lesson of Local Management of Schools (LMS) needs no heavy type.

Getting the timing right

Governors complain that they are always asked to comment on things when it's too late. Either the event has already happened or the paper is so shiny and perfect that it seems rude to ask questions. I wouldn't belittle the task of getting the timing right, but one very simple tactic is to start a meeting with a run-through of what is going to come up before meeting again, so that governors can plan how they are going to organise themselves, and the school reminds itself to weave some of their thinking processes into its own. It will work if professionals can modify their admirable perfectionism, consult at sketch plan stage, not be too proud to ask questions when they don't know the answers, and think aloud in public.

Getting the level right

Governors mustn't meddle. They are less likely to do so if they feel secure in their ownership of strategic decisions. The governor who comes into a reading lesson and interferes unhelpfully will not be the one who has discussed reading policy. Neither is the governor who finds it hard to accept a school's decision on a pupil misdemeanour likely to be the one who took part in a discussion of behaviour policy with staff. But professionals must play the game too and not breach, in the name of day-to-day management, policies which they have shared at governor level. For instance, they should not decide against advertising the special needs vacancy when governors decided to strengthen special needs when possible. They should not cancel the whole year's treat because a few wrongdoers wouldn't own up, if their governors have a policy of not punishing the innocent. If heads are governors they should not in any case offend against corporate loyalty, even in a battle they have lost.

Encouraging good teamwork

There should be no governing bodies with A and B teams. That means good and careful induction of new members, sharing the work and information effectively and equitably, and trying hard not to work more closely with those governors who are easier to work with.

- Watch the relationship with the chairperson. It can be close, confiding and warm, but should never exclude others. The chairperson has no legal status to act on behalf of governors except (a) when specifically asked to do so on a matter which can legally be delegated or (b) in a dire emergency. The logic of the law is a chairperson who is more of a teambuilder, consulter, work planner. Yes, the keeper of the vision. Yes, the megaphone for the school. Yes, the head's frank adviser. And the governors' voice, perhaps, but not their head or hands.

- Keep a running audit of skills and talents in the team and use them. But make it clear you mean skills ordinary people have – organising, listening, peacemaking. Not just accountancy or word-processing.

- Make sure all interest groups are spread over all committees.

- Make sure all information is shared – mistrust is destructive.

- Be watchful for diffident members and encourage them.

- Promote good delegation and work-sharing. Break up the paper mountain – one unopened brown envelope per governor, distributed randomly. Let them bring it back at once if it's urgent, if not find out if it's for information, action or comment, present it to governors and take follow-up action.

- Help teacher and parent governors to fulfil their representative (not delegative) role of communicating and reporting back. Try to be relaxed about communication which isn't channelled through you. It won't hurt you.

- Finally, know the working-together rules and try to ensure they are kept. Good rules protect the unpowerful. Most rules for governors are good rules.

Table 4.1.2 *Tips for good teamwork*

Involving governors in the school

The lump in the throat which governors get from the harvest festival or the school play is important – it keeps them going. But it doesn't actually help them make better decisions. There must be a system for each and every governor to get into classrooms regularly. It could be a 'governor of the month' with each governor on duty for one month of the school year, fixed well ahead – planting the tree, giving out the cycling proficiency badges, helping appoint the teacher, looking at some manageable bit of the school's work. Or it could be an attachment to a subject – sport, the arts, special needs – or a class or year. As far as peer group pressure (public shame) can prevent it, no backsliding must be allowed. The governors *will* the arrangement. Involvement must be reported. Every system needs managing. Encourage teachers to share their enthusiasms with governors – they need ambassadors.

4.2

Appointing Staff

Brian Unwin

The task of appointing staff has always been of crucial importance, for the quality and commitment of staff is vital in ensuring that the whole curriculum is effectively provided for pupils. Staffing accounts for upwards of 80 per cent of the budget in most schools, so good, thorough and well-thought-through procedures are essential.

The Education Reform Act of 1988 made significant changes in the powers and responsibilities of governing bodies in this respect and, together with School Government Regulations 1989 and 1991, established the legal framwork.

Legal requirements

For maintained schools, where the governors are the 'relevant body', two documents must guide and inform their arrangements for making appointments to the school (including the appointment of external candidates, internal appointments and promotions).

First, there is Schedule 3 of ERA 1988. This schedule sets out the requirements for:

- the appointment of headteachers and deputy headteachers, including the arrangements and composition of the selection panel and its relationship with the whole governing body and the requirement to advertise;

- the appointment of other teachers, including the occasions when an advertisement is required; the position of candidates nominated by the Local Education Authority (LEA); the requirement, provided the selected candidate is qualified, for the LEA to appoint the selected person;

- the power for the governors to delegate the function of appointment to one or more governors, to the headteacher, or to one or more governors and the headteacher acting together;

- the advice of the chief education officer (CEO) and the head-teacher, including the entitlement to be present at *all* pro-cedures to give advice; in the case of headship and deputy headship appointments, it is the duty of the CEO to give advice whether asked or not; in other appointments, the duty is to give advice if so requested. The governing body or delegated individuals or group must consider that advice. It is critical that such consideration should be clearly minuted and, if rejected, reasons given. On this may rest the success of the defence of acting in good faith;

- appointments of non-teaching staff, including consideration of matters to be sent on to the LEA, the consultation with the head;

- the appointment of clerk to the governing body.

Second, there is the School Government Regulations 1989 (Statu-tory Instrument 1503) and School Government Regulations 1991 (Statutory Instrument 2854). If the governing body choose to make appointments by using the arrangements outlined in Regulations 25 and 26, they must make those arrangements according to the detailed procedures that are required, remembering that a quorum of two-thirds of the full governing body is required to establish the committees and their remits.

It is under Regulation 25 that the governing body will determine its policies relating to matters of appointment procedures (determi-nation of the delegation to individuals or groups, grades, etc).

Governors of *aided* and *grant-maintained* schools have their own regulations that inform their procedures.

Guidelines for making appointments

The School Development Plan

In effect, this will be the strategic plan for the school for the next few years, containing short- to long-term arrangements. It is likely to include a view of staffing structures and grades appropriate to the functions and priorities set out in the structure.

The governors' policy on pay

This establishes the governing body's intention to be a good employer and addresses the issues of recruitment, retention, promotion and professional development. This policy should be in sufficient detail to establish criteria for grades, recruitment points on the standard scale, and the appropriate point on the spine for heads and deputies. It should set out criteria for each of the six considerations set out in the current Teachers' Pay and Conditions document (1993) that establishes the 18-point pay spine: qualifications, experience, responsibilities, excellence, recruitment and retention, and special educational needs. For non-teaching staff, refer to the appropriate pay scales and advisory documents from Local Authorities' Conditions of Service Advisory Board.

Governors' employment powers

Two circulars on Local Management of Schools – DES 7/88 – 'Education Reform Act: Local Management of Schools' (paragraphs 157–164) and DES 7/91 – 'Local Management of Schools: Further Guidance' (paragraphs 46–48) – set out the following duties and responsibilities of the governing body in relation to appointments:

- to set the number of staff employed (teaching and non-teaching);
- to establish the appropriate procedures for appointments within the regulations;
- to appoint and determine salary levels within the arrangements set out in the relevant national agreements; and
- to use, as they determine, any discretions that the governing body have.

Heads and deputies need to ensure that they are familiar with the framework and details of the policy, procedures, powers and responsibilities that exist and particularly the relationship between the governing body and the LEA who holds and services the contracts of staff.

In making appointments, the governing body must be made aware of their responsibilities to observe the requirements of legislation on:

- Race Relations Act 1976
- Equal Pay Act 1970
- Sex Discrimination Act 1975
- Trade Union and Labour Relations Act 1974

In the matters so far discussed, the governing bodies of independent and grant-maintained and aided schools will follow their own precise rules that govern the application of employment principals.

Annual staffing review

In order that decisions on staffing are made with the most up-to-date information, a formal review should take place each year so that the pupil numbers and curriculum needs can be analysed and compared to the existing staff and curriculum. Informed decisions on staffing levels, particularly on whether vacancies that occur should be recruited on the basis of a new job specification, can then be made. This has to be matched against the budget. This exercise will reveal the need to:

- make additional appointments and the nature of those appointments;

- fill a vacancy in a different curriculum area; or

- reduce the number of staff employed.

Stages of appointment and preparatory steps required

- vacancy analysis

- job description and postholder specification – effective potential salary costs

- framing the advertisement

- shortlisting

- arrangements for interview

- interview questions

- offer of the post and confirmation of offer

- information to the LEA

Table 4.2.1 *Stages of appointment summary*

Preparation

Have the following materials ready for use:

1. *application forms* setting out information that will help heads and deputies to establish basic salary costs and to establish the correlation with the job specification;

2. *declaration forms* for spent convictions for shortlisted candidates where they will have close contact with children;

3. *school information and specifications* to be sent to candidates.

Vacancy analysis

Establish whether the head should do this alone or with a committee.

Considerations

Conclusions from the staffing review need to be clearly understood with regard to the nature of the vacancy.

Questions

What are the staffing priorities of the school? What jobs need doing? Should the vacancy be advertised as direct replacement? Should it be a different post? If so, what? Or, should it not be filled at all?

Decision

If a decision is made to recruit, then proceed to the advertisement.

Advertisement

- Keep content short and to the point, requesting prospective candidates to send for further details;

- pay attention to style. Is there a standard format to be followed? Is there a logo?;

- establish a closing date and who is to handle applications. Is a reference number required on applications?;

- prepare the following materials to be sent to applicants:
  - job specification;
  - postholder specification;
  - information on school: size, ethos expectation, aims and objectives, and organisation.

113

Establishing the job specification

This could be either specific to a subject or department, eg history, or generic, such as head of year; with the year, department or faculty specified. It is helpful to divide the specification into three parts:

1. the main responsibilities;

2. additional specific responsibilities; and

3. general duties and responsibilities that are shared with other staff.

With reference to these areas, the post title and scale should be fully set out. Each of the responsibilities should include the following items:

- to whom responsible;

- responsibility for other staff;

- responsibility for rooms, equipment, finance, etc;

- responsibility for pupils;

- training and staff development;

- other relevant details;

- pastoral duties;

- administration duties; and

- supervisory duties (general).

General duties and responsibilities should appear. These cover the duties and responsibilities of all staff.

Preparation for interviews

This involves careful thought and preparation of questions to be asked. Who will ask them? Who will lead the interviews? Are there to be other techniques utilised? These will need thorough preparation:

- in-tray exercises

- analysis of a school problem

- taking a staff meeting or a committee
- simulations, etc.

Post-holder specification

```
Experience sought:
   – type of school
   – age of pupils
   – length of teaching experience
Qualifications:
   – specific subject/academic
   – general
   – phase
   – INSET updating
Skills/Knowledge:
   – listed as required
```

Table 4.2.2 *Post-holder specification*

This specification must be written carefully so as not to discriminate against any one in relation to gender, race or pay.

Short list

It is good practice for this to be done by the head, together with the people who will form the appointing group. How many candidates would you ideally invite to interview? What is the cost of that? Are you going to have a long list and reduce to a short list after seeking referees, or are you going directly to a short list for interview? At interview, how are references to be used, taking into account local practices or policies on use of references (ie open or confidential)?

Criteria
You have already established these by the job and postholder specification. Which candidates best match the criteria?

References
Are you going to send a general request or ask specific questions? Enclose the job specification. Is the practice in your area to send for references after selection or to use open references only?

Invitation to candidates

This will give: details of date, time and place; details of the arrangements for the interview; directions to location of the interview; and an indication of expenses that are recoverable.

Interview

The schedule of visits and appointment with projected timings should include:

- an opportunity for the candidates to see the school;
- a meeting with the head/deputies and relevant staff;
- the time of interview, and/or exercises.

With regard to physical setting, care must be taken over the:

- choice of room for the interview and its layout; and
- the arrangement of the room for candidates awaiting interview.

In planning interviews/exercises, care should be taken to:

- create an atmosphere that puts candidates at ease;
- establish the procedure to be used;
- give papers/summaries of candidates' details to interviewing panel;
- brief the interview panel on their task, referring to the specifications and criteria;
- establish questions to be asked so that each candidate is treated similarly;
- balance types of questions – open, closed, multiple, hypothetical, those requiring self-assessment;
- ask questions in logical order;
- discuss the nature and extent of supplementary follow-up questions;
- establish that questions relative to gender, race, religion, political or trade union affiliation, or of a personal family nature, are not permitted, as these could lead to litigation or process in one form or another;
- give an opportunity for candidates to ask questions to the interviewing committee. *Remember* that candidates may wish to establish clearly at which point of the pay spine they will be paid. Information must be on hand to answer such questions.

Decision

The decision-making process should involve:

- discussion on each criterion;

- systematic discussion of each candidate by the people who are directly involved in the process;

- selection of one candidate who best matches the crtieria;

- the process of selection, either consensus in open discussion or voting (open or secret ballot);

- notifying the successful candidate – and agreement on who tells the unsuccessful;

- arranging a de-briefing for the unsuccessful candidate if this has been agreed.

The following procedure should be followed for confirmation of verbal offer of post in writing:

1. letter to candidate – stating post, salary, start date and confirmation of job specification;

2. letter to LEA, if relevant, giving photocopy or original of application form, together with any accompanying letter of application and any disclosure of spent/unspent convictions.

Remember that this documentation establishes the contract, which is critical for independent, aided and grant-maintained schools. Remember that the Trade Union Reform and Employment Rights Act 1993 (TURERA) has reduced to *two* months the time after the commencement of employment that the employer has to give a detailed statement of employment particulars to the employee. Governing bodies that are the direct employer should familiarise themselves with the provision.

Summary and further considerations

The establishment of policies, procedures and processes that are known and understood by the existing staff of the school and by external candidates provides the firmest foundation for making effective appointments to the staff of the school, primarily because the principles, concepts and thought processes are embodied in the procedures.

The additional bonus is that the danger of falling foul of any complaint under the sex, race or equal opportunities legislation and of any grievance on pay or promotion will have been significantly lessened, if not completely prevented. Certainly such complaints and grievances can be more completely answered if the procedures are fully followed. Each stage can be evidenced by the record made at the time.

Even more positively, accurate procedures that select effectively are cost-effective, in spite of the need for thoroughness and hence expenditure of time.

Staffing: Pay and Conditions of Service

Peter Downes

The most significant changes brought in by the 1993 Pay and Conditions Document from those of the two previous years were:

- to remove all the previous discretionary and incentive allowances and to bring all teachers on to a Common Pay Spine (CPS) of 18 points;

- to increase the responsibility of governors by requiring them to make an annual review of the pay of all teachers, heads and deputies;

- to continue the move towards performance related pay (PRP) by requiring governors to give an incremental enhancement only to those whose performance has been judged satisfactory, and by emphasising the benefits of rewarding teachers with extra money for classroom excellence.

Transitional arrangements

Moving from one system of payments to another is never easy. In the case of the 1993 Document, problems arose from the irregularity of the steps between the points on the CPS, causing some young teachers who were holding the previous incentive allowances to find themselves disadvantaged. Cash safeguarding was introduced to protect them, granting extra sums to make their salaries equal to what they would have had under the 1992 Document. As some teachers will still be 'underpaid' in September 1994, it is not yet clear how they will continue to be protected.

The other main area of difficulty was the Inner London Supplement (ILS). The School Teachers Review Body (STRB) originally intended the ILS of £822 to be replaced by an extra point on the CPS. It was pointed out to them and the DFE that this would bring serious funding problems to most inner London schools and a concession was made whereby the ILS was cash protected at the £822 figure. Whether this special arrangement will continue into 1994 is another issue which remains to be resolved by the 1994 Document.

Governors' responsibilities

The need for governors to produce a clear pay policy is even greater than ever. They must:

1. set up a staffing personnel committee of, say, five members;

2. approve the pay policy drawn up by the staffing committee and delegate its implementation to that committee, or if it so decides, to the head and chairman of governors reporting to that committee;

3. set up an appeals panel of not fewer than three governors who are *not* on the staffing committee so they can judge on appeals without prior knowledge of the issues and prejudice.

The staffing committee's remit

The staffing committee must:

1. formulate the pay policy (probably following the models and advice provided by the LEA or one of the teacher associations), making sure that the implications of the policy are fully understood by all members of the committee. (It is good practice to consult the representatives of the unions and associations at the draft stage);

2. decide the level of staffing after receiving guidance from the curriculum committee;

3. place all teachers annually on the CPS according to the criteria mentioned below;

4. draw up an advertising and appointing system (specifying the extent to which the head and chair of governors have flexibility to act);

5. ensure that a disciplinary procedure is in place and, in extreme cases, dismiss a member of staff, following the code of practice very carefully and drawing on external advice if in any doubt;

6. receive reports from the head (or deputy) on the appraisal procedure (but not to have direct access to the appraisal reports themselves);

7. do whatever it can to provide all the staff with reasonable working conditions and to reassure them that they are 'good employers' ie have due regard to Equal Opportunities, staff welfare etc.

The pay policy

The main section of the pay policy will be a definition of the criteria by which the staffing committee intends to carry out its annual review and its placement of teachers on the CPS. Teachers accumulate points under the following headings:

Points for qualifications

Two points are awarded for those holding a good honours degree. Other teachers start at point 0 (NB unlike the previous system where teachers started at point 1).

Points for experience

1. Experience outside teaching can be recognised if it is relevant to the teacher's skills in the appointment. It is usual to allow one point for every two/three years of relevant experience.

2. Experience within teaching is recognised by a point for every year successfully completed (a year equals a teaching commitment of whatever length for 26 weeks or more, so part-timers also qualify for a full annual experience point).

3. The maximum number of points under this heading is 9 (or 7 for those who have a good honours degree). This means that point 9 is in effect the top of the salary scale for those who have no entitlements under any other heading.

4. A point for experience can be withheld if the governors take the view, as advised by the head, that the teacher's performance has been unsatisfactory. It is strongly recommended that heads do not make an adverse recommendation without having invoked the normal disciplinary proceedings in the course of the year.

Points for responsibilities

Up to 5 points can be awarded for extra responsibilities (head of year, head of department etc). It is essential that any points awarded under this heading should be accompanied by a clear job definition which will also state whether the points are permanent or temporary, and to whom the post-holder is responsible for the satisfactory fulfilment of their role.

The governors also have the difficult task of deciding how many points to award under this heading. (There used to be guideline parameters but these were removed from the 1993 Document.) In practice, this will require negotiations between staffing, curriculum and finance committees as the head seeks to put in place the structure needed to run the school within the financial constraints of the school as a whole. For a fuller discussion of this issue, see 'Where's the incentive?' in *Managing Schools Today*, vol 2, No 8.

Points for excellence

Up to 3 points can be awarded for outstanding performance, an ill-defined concept but one to which the government is strongly attached. They see these awards as going mainly to those classroom teachers who perform outstandingly well and who do not wish to seek financial improvement by taking on responsibilities which will remove them from classroom contact with children. Anecdotal evidence suggests that most governors are fighting shy of using these points, partly because there are many other pressures on the school budget and also because they are anxious not to demotivate those who do not qualify for such payments, worthy though they may be.

Points for recruitment and retention

Up to 2 points are available to attract or retain teachers in shortage subjects, the exact definition of which will vary from place to place and year to year. An award under this heading has to be reviewed every two years and if the teacher shortage which provoked the original award has eased, the points could be removed. Most governors seem to be treating this heading with as much caution as the 'excellence' heading.

Points for special needs

A teacher in a special school has a mandatory entitlement to one point and a second point may be awarded where the teacher's experience and qualifications enhance the value of the work being undertaken. This enables teachers previously holding a B allowance to continue to have two points on the new CPS.

Teachers in mainstream schools who wholly or mainly teach pupils with statements of special needs may also qualify. The practice which appears to be emerging is for those who teach in support of statemented children in a mainstream classroom to not be given these points. Qualified teachers of the deaf and the blind, previously entitled to an allowance of £702, have that converted to an extra point in the assimilation process.

A policy will need to be put in place for the salaries of the head and deputies. The main factor will be the size of the job as determined by the total points of the school, which is related to the ranges of groups 1 to 6. In addition, the governors may decide to enhance the salary of the head and deputies by moving them up the scale on the following criteria:

- any special responsibilities in the post;

- the social, economic or cultural background of the pupils;

- the difficulty of filling the post;

- the sustained overall performance which appreciably exceeds that normally expected.

In practice, about 25 per cent of heads and deputies have been moved up from their 1991 assimilation point, but only a third of those have been enhanced on the basis of the fourth criterion. It is particularly difficult for governors to apply performance criteria to the head and deputies while refusing them to the rest of the teachers.

Trends

Apart from the wider question of a freeze on public sector pay awards, the two main issues which will be debated for the 1994 settlement are:

1. Should the CPS be amended to make it more manageable? A longer pay spine of equal steps would make it easier to solve some of the problems of assimilation and unequal pay which have emerged from the 1993 Document.

2. Will PRP become mandatory? DFE evidence indicates that the government see PRP as a means of raising standards and would like to see it introduced, even in a time of overall pay restraint. Depending on how hawkish they are, this could well become the next battleground between the government and the teaching profession.

Further reading

School Teachers' Pay and Conditions Document (1993) DFE.
Circular 8/93, DFE.
Croner's School Governors Manual, Section 7, Croner Publications.
Guidance on the 1993 Pay Award, Secondary Heads Association.

4.4

School-based Initial Teacher Education

Donald McIntyre and Geoff Rhodes

One of the most recent extra responsibilities which the government has asked schools to undertake is a very much larger role in the initial professional education of teachers. There is much that can be welcomed in principle about this initiative. In practice, it confronts school managements with some difficult decisions.

Should the school get involved?

The biggest decision is the first one, about whether and on what terms the school should get involved at all in taking responsibility for initial teacher education. It can be considered from a number of perspectives:

- **The 'altruistic' perspective**: is the school well placed and willing to take on responsibility for preparing **good** new teachers? If the school is to set high standards for itself, then the task will be a complex and demanding one. This perspective is altruistic only, of course, in the sense that 'charity begins at home': schools will be the first to reap the benefits of a generation of good new teachers, and the first to bear the costs of shoddy initial training.

- **The financial perspective**: substantial sums of money are on offer to schools for undertaking this work. It is tempting to view this as extra income, for a task that will require only a modest proportion of it. The truth, however, is that most teachers who accept responsibilities for initial teacher education find it necessary to give large amounts of time to caring for the student teachers and to ensuring that they learn the difficult lessons necessary for them to become effective teachers. Local management has reinforced the fact that teacher time is the most expensive as well as the most valuable resource of any school. Headteachers have to ensure that their schools acquire the increased resources necessary for undertaking such work; but, even more, they have to ensure that these extra resources go to giving time for the extra work and therefore that pupils benefit rather than lose from the school's involvement. The easy option of 'creative accounting' can quickly lead to staff demoralisation and burn-out or to parental complaints.

- **The type of scheme under consideration**: for the foreseeable future, schools are likely to have three main types of initial teacher education scheme on offer:

  1. Schemes run by the school, on its own or in a consortium with other schools.

     In this kind of scheme, schools have to take on the substantial administrative, planning and co-ordinating functions hitherto fulfiled by universities, as well as developing their own distinctive professional education functions. Engagement in such schemes is likely, in our view, to be wasteful, inefficient and dangerously distracting for schools and very unlikely to lead to high quality initial teacher education.

  2. Schemes run by higher education institutions (HEIs), with schools being paid for hosting individual student teachers on a one-off basis.

     Such schemes make the least demands on schools, but they also make it impossible for schools to plan efficiently for the work. In particular, staff cannot be timetabled for it in a planned way without properly timetabled time for mentoring, attention to student teachers is likely to be adequate only through the use of supply teaching, with all the negative consequences that that brings for pupils. In addition, the HE component of such schemes cannot take account of the school's ideas and concerns, and there is a great danger of incoherence.

  3. Partnership schemes planned and run jointly with one or more HEIs and with other schools.

     Such schemes, avoiding as they can the problems of both the other types, are in our view likely to offer the most satisfactory approach to school-based initial teacher education. This does not mean, of course, that all partnership schemes are well-conceived; each has to be considered on its merits.

- **The developmental perspective**: in deciding whether or not to engage in initial teacher education, a school has to consider not only what is on offer, but also the school's own needs and potential. Can the scheme be made beneficial for the school? What can the school do with the scheme, not only for the student teachers but also to help itself develop? The answers to these questions will depend not only on the scheme but also on the school's, and its several departments' state of readiness to implement and use the scheme. For example, the staff's profile of experience will be important in this.

What roles and responsibilities are involved?

Initial teacher education should be a **whole-school responsibility**. It is when the task is treated as one for the school as a whole, and undertaken on a sufficient scale and given sufficient significance for that to make sense, that it is likely to be done well and to benefit the school. Good school-based initial teacher education will impinge on most aspects of a school's life – not only classroom teaching but also pastoral work, development and evaluation activities, internal and external communication systems, extracurricular activities, staffrooms and staff social life. (A wise school management team will therefore ensure that the decision to get involved is one made by the whole staff.)

The Professional Tutor role

Because initial teacher education is a whole-school responsibility, there has to be one key person who co-ordinates it throughout the school. In Oxfordshire schools, that person is given the title of Professional Tutor and that is the term we use here. The Professional Tutor should:

- be a member of the senior management team to ensure that initial teacher education can be treated as a significant task, to be co-ordinated effectively with other aspects of the school's work;

- have as his or her primary task that of leading the school's initial teacher education team, supporting and guiding other members of the team;

127

- negotiate on behalf of the school with HEIs and other schools involved in the scheme, and be the main channel of communication;

- probably also have responsibility for the induction of newly-qualified teachers (NQTs) and other new teachers, also perhaps for other professional development work within the school, and be a member of the INSET Committee;

- personally have an educational role in running a programme of whole-school and cross-curricular studies for the school's student teachers, and in involving other members of staff in the programme;

- co-ordinate student teachers' practical education in relation to teachers' tutorial roles;

- accept substantial responsibility for attending to student teachers' personal welfare, their difficulties in coming to terms with 'being a teacher', any problems in their relationships with their mentors, and any friction with other members of staff (most likely because of conflicting expectations);

- accept considerable assessment responsibilities, including acting as a moderator for assessments made by other members of the team;

- monitor the impact of the school's initial teacher education work on the pupils, to ensure that none are over-exposed to student teachers and that none are disadvantaged by the school's involvement in this work.

The mentor role

Essential, complex and demanding as the Professional Tutor's role is, arguably the most important initial teacher education role within the school is that of the mentor, the teacher who takes responsibility for the learning activities of one or more student teachers in relation to classroom teaching. In secondary schools, the clearest and most appropriate division of labour is for mentors to have full responsibility for the management of student teachers' learning activities within their subject departments and for the Professional Tutor to have responsibility for extra-departmental activities.

Mentors need to use a variety of strategies and to take account of many considerations in helping student teachers at different stages in their learning to teach. The role is a time-consuming one, and one which requires the development of skills and understandings not generally used by classroom teachers. It also depends on making informed and intelligent judgements about fruitful ways in which student teachers might work with subject colleagues and their classes, and sensitivity in negotiating such arrangements with colleagues. This is not, however, the place to elaborate on the complexities of the task of mentoring (but see McIntyre et al, 1993; Hagger et al, 1993). From the perspective of school management, the three important issues are:

- ensuring that mentors have satifactory conditions to enable them to do their task effectively; this implies that
  (i)   only departments well placed to take on initial teacher education should be involved in any particular year (eg not overwhelmed by other demands, stable staffing, most teachers quite experienced);
  (ii) as already noted, adequate time is set aside by the school for the work of mentoring;
  (iii) there is a supportive head of department;
  (iv) support is also available from the professional tutor;
  (v)   there are strong links with the HEI tutors responsible for the subject area, and effective joint planning with them.

- being clear about the criteria and procedures for appointing mentors; among considerations which should normally be relevant are:
  (i)   the head of department's views about the development of the department and about the appropriateness of different teachers for the role;
  (ii) the teaching competence and experience of possible candidates;
  (iii) the attitudes of possible candidates to teaching, in particular their readiness to accept that there can be more than one right way, and their belief in the learnability and teachability of classroom teaching abilities;
  (iv) the attitudes of possible candidates to student teachers, and in particular their appreciation of the distinctive needs of adult learners;
  (v)   any views held by collaborating HEI staff about the appropriateness of different teachers for the role;
  (vi) the reputation of possible candidates among their departmental colleagues.

- developing adequate quality assurance procedures to ensure that the job is done well and to the benefit of the school; this will be discussed in the next section of this paper.

The division of labour with higher education

Roles and responsibilities within the school depend heavily on arrangements made in partnership with HEIs. Three aspects of these arrangements may be identified as especially important:

- **The nature of the school's expected contribution**: whatever the agreed division of labour, good initial teacher education will involve school staff in considerable work, and in the development of new skills and understandings. This can be kept within bounds, however, if the emphasis is placed squarely on student teachers learning from the expertise which school staff use in practice, from understanding the actual practices and policies of the school and its staff, and of course from engaging, with the support of teachers, in the teaching of pupils. More abstract, generalised and library-based learning should more appropriately be the responsibility of HEI staff.

- **Effective flow of information**: the tasks of school-based teacher educators are made considerably easier if they can rely on knowing what the student teachers at any stage have and have not studied elsewhere, and in what terms.

- **Partnership in decision-making**: school-based teacher educators can undertake their work with much greater confidence if they can be sure of having a significant say in deciding what the student teachers are to be expected to do, both in the schools and in the HEI, and if they can be confident that all important decisions about the programme will be taken jointly.

Maximising benefits and minimising costs

Engagement in initial teacher education can bring substantial benefits but can also carry considerable costs. Management teams will be concerned to maximise the former and to minimise the latter.

Costs

Some costs are unnecessary and damaging, others are inevitable, and some are well worth undertaking as investments likely to produce future benefits. Possible costs include:

- less effective pupil learning, a cost which is not at all necessary and which can be completely avoided through effective mentoring; but without thoughtful planning and monitoring, the presence of several student teachers in the school over long periods could be very damaging in this way.

- time and energy spent on student teachers, the major necessary cost: in well designed schemes, time spent appropriately with student teachers at early stages will generally lead to rich benefits for the school later; but mentoring in particular can be very time-consuming and mentors have to be able to control their allocation of time judiciously.

- time spent at meetings for partnership planning, and also for the school's initial teacher education team, can also be a valuable investment leading to substantial benefits, provided that meetings are efficiently prepared and conducted.

- extra complications for the whole school staff are inevitable, but will be a very minor cost if there has been adequate initial consultation and if the professional tutor manages the scheme skilfully.

- divisiveness within and among departments is a possible cost, with people using initial teacher education to develop their own empires and not contributing to other teams; this cost can be avoided with careful appointing of mentors and with thoughtfulness about the range of subject departments involved at any time.

- direct financial costs should be relatively small, but need to be budgeted for; for example, student teachers tend to do a lot of photocopying of materials.

Benefits

The opportunity to contribute to the development of their profession is something which many teachers value. There can also, however, be direct benefits to the school itself from engagement in initial teacher education. Possible benefits include:

- for individual teachers, especially mentors, enhanced job satisfaction through the emphasis given to skills of classroom teaching, and to **their** skills in particular;

- for mentors, opportunities for professional development through taking a leadership role within their subject departments, a role which offers excellent preparation for that of head of department;

- for subject departments, revitalisation of the work of the department as a result of:
  - the presence of new enthusiastic teachers not burdened by recent educational history;
  - the encouragement to look afresh at the department's established ways of teaching;
  - networking with other mentors and with HEI staff, bringing fresh approaches and new resources;

- also for subject departments, the availability, especially towards the end of student teachers' school-based work, of an increased number of competent classroom practitioners, thus allowing (a) increased attention for individual pupils, and (b) release of teachers to do other work;

- for the Professional Tutor, a stimulus for fresh thinking about the school's provision for NQTs and other new teachers;

- also for the Professional Tutor, an opportunity to give various teachers within the school a chance to share their expertise and to develop their own sense of worth, through engagement in the whole-school programme;

- for the school as a whole, an opportunity to identify and to recruit good new staff in shortage areas;

- also for the school as a whole, the opportunity to enhance its image through asserting its status as a school recognised as competent to train new teachers.

Quality assurance

The quality of a school's contributions to initial teacher education, and of the schemes in which they participate, must of course be judged mainly in terms of the quality of student teachers' learning experiences and of their learning outcomes. Schools will also, however, properly be concerned to assure themselves that the benefits outlined above are being maximised, and the costs minimised.

The process of quality assurance will be greatly facilitated where the partnership between schools and HEIs is robust enough for each to offer the others an honest, critical commentary on the strengths and weaknesses of its contributions. Self-appraisal, feedback from the student teachers, and commentaries from visiting OFSTED teams will be other important inputs to the quality assurance process. During this period when schools are being asked to contribute to radically new arrangements for initial teacher education, it is obviously especially important that quality assurance should be given a high priority.

Conclusion

Faced with the opportunity to engage substantially in initial teacher education, each school has to think hard and realistically about what it has to offer, what it has to gain, and what it has to lose. Only when a school is confident that it has something valuable to offer and something valuable to gain should it commit itself to this extra work.

Furthermore, one should not assume that the benefits a school can offer or those that it can gain will remain the same over a period of years. It may well be appropriate for many schools to participate in initial teacher education for a limited period and then to take a break, allowing others to contribute and to benefit.

References

Hagger, H, Burn, K and McIntyre, D (1993) *The School Mentor Handbook*, London: Kogan Page.

McIntyre, D, Hagger, H and Wilkin, M (1993) (eds) *Mentoring: Perspective on School-based Teacher Education* London: Kogan Page.

4.5

Staff Appraisal

Ken Biggs

The historical context

Appraisal schemes were introduced into individual schools and
LEAs in the late 1970s. The first DES funded study was in Suffolk
LEA in the early 1980s. In 1986, an ACAS working party report
recommended that a pilot project be set up as a precursor of a
national appraisal scheme. The DES funded pilot projects from 1987
to 1989 in six LEAs – Croydon, Cumbria, Newcastle, Salford,
Somerset and Suffolk. Those involved in this project reported to a
National Steering Group (NSG) which included representatives
from the DES, LEAs, Teacher and Headteacher Associations. The
NSG Report was published in 1989.

After a period of consultation and proposals for a voluntary
framework, regulations for a national scheme were included in 'The
Education (School Teacher Appraisal) Regulations 1991'.

Purposes of appraisal

In the ACAS report, appraisal was understood to be a 'continuous
and systematic process intended to help individual teachers with
their professional development and career planning'.

The 1991 Regulations include a number of specific aims. They are
to:

- recognise the achievements of teachers and help them to
  identify ways of improving their skills and performance;

- help teachers, governing bodies and local education authorities to determine whether a change of duties would help teachers' professional development and improve their career prospects;

- identify teachers' potential for career development, with the aim of helping them, where possible, through appropriate in-service training;

- help teachers having difficulties with their performance, through appropriate guidance, counselling and training;

- inform those responsible for providing references for teachers;

- improve the management of schools.

The 1991 Regulations on teacher appraisal

The Regulations require an appraising body to be responsible for all aspects of appraisal in the Regulations. The appraising body will be the LEA for its own schools, and for grant-maintained schools the governing body will be the appraising body.

The governing body of all schools has a duty to ensure that appraisal arrangements are carried out and that they are kept informed of its progress by reports from the headteacher. These reports should include a summary of the teachers' targets for action, and the progress in achieving these targets.

The Regulations apply to all qualified teachers in maintained schools except for:

- those with contracts of less than one year;

- those employed for less than 40 per cent of full time;

- probationary teachers;

- articled, licensed or unqualified teachers;

- advisory or specialist peripatetic staff.

The appraising body must meet the following targets:

- at least half the teachers for whom it was responsible on 1 September 1991 must complete the first year of the appraisal cycle by the end of the summer term of 1993;

- all the teachers for whom it was responsible on 1 September 1991 must complete the first year of the cycle by the end of the summer term of 1995;

- all teachers who were not the responsibility of the appraising body on 1 September 1991 should start their first appraisal cycle on or before the start of the 1995/96 academic year.

The Regulations require the following:

- classroom observation;
- an appraisal interview;
- an appraisal statement;
- a review meeting.

They also suggest an initial meeting; a self appraisal by the teacher; and collection of data from sources other than classroom observations.

Stages in setting up an appraisal process

Preparing for appraisal

The appraisal of teachers and headteachers cannot stand in isolation. Appraisal must be relevant to the development needs of the school and to the professional development of the individual teacher. Appraisal should therefore relate to the agreed objectives of the school and to the individual teacher's role in achieving these. All teachers should have job descriptions and time budgets to provide the context for effective appraisal.

The Regulations specify that the headteacher shall appoint the appraisers for each teacher in the school. Teachers should not be permitted to choose their appraiser but heads should not unreasonably refuse requests from teachers for alternative appraisers. Many schools have found it desirable to have a common training for all staff whether for appraisee or appraiser, so that all staff are fully aware of the process being undertaken.

Such training could well include detailed school agreements on the process, specifying such matters as timing and staff cover in addition to any agreements fixed by the appraising body.

Initial meeting and self-appraisal

An initial meeting and/or self-appraisal are not compulsory but fulfil many worthwhile functions.

An initial meeting can:

- confirm the purpose and clarify the context of the appraisal;
- consider the scope and agree a focus for the appraisal;

- agree arrangements for classroom observation and/or other data collection;

- agree the final timetable for the process.

Self-appraisal offers the opportunity to:

- reflect on current practice and review objectives;

- celebrate success and consider development needs;

- examine knowledge and skills that could be utilised by the school.

Observation and data collection

Teachers will normally be observed while teaching on two or more occasions and for a total of at least one hour. Classroom observation is a very complex skill. It is likely to be successful if there are:

- clear criteria agreed in advance;

- agreed methods to collect and interpret data.

Information recorded should concentrate on:

- providing descriptions rather judgements;

- giving information rather than advice;

- giving specific rather than generalised examples of what was seen.

It may be desirable to meet very soon after each lesson observation to provide a brief feedback. The Circular on Appraisal includes a Code of Practice as an appendix.

The appraisal interview

The appraisal interview is the key stage of the whole process. It is important that conditions are carefully arranged so that there is privacy and sufficient time to facilitate fruitful discussion.
 The interview should involve:

- further clarification, if necessary, of the teacher's job description;

- a review of the work done, successes and areas for development identified since the previous appraisal;

- discussion of professional development needs to help appraisees undertake their current jobs even better and to prepare them for their next post;

- discussion of career development as appropriate;

- discussion of the appraisee's role in, and contribution to, the policies and management of the school, and any constraints placed on the appraisee's work by the school context;

- identification of targets for future action and development;

- decisions about what actions are to be taken by the appraisee and appraiser and how targets are to be achieved;

- clarification of points to be included in the appraisal statement.

The appraisal statement

The appraisal statement must include:

- an agreed record of the discussions in the appraisal interview;

- a separate action plan including targets agreed for action and details of how these are to be achieved.

The Regulations allow the appraisee, within 20 working days of receiving the statement, to add comments in writing.

The appraisal statements are confidential documents. Only the appraiser, appraisee and the headteacher should have copies of the statements. The Chief Education Officer also has the right to request a copy of an individual statement.

The headteacher, on request, may supply the chair of governors with the target sheet for an individual teacher. The chair does not have the right to see the full statement.

The governing body may see a non-attributable aggregate of targets for all teachers but not any part of an individual teacher's statement.

Appraisal statements should normally remain on file for two appraisal cycles, ie for a maximum of four years. It should include plans for a review and for a formal review meeting during the year following the appraisal.

Appraisal Statements or any part of the process may not form part of any disciplinary or dismissal procedure.

Monitoring and evaluation

Each school will need to make adequate arrangements for the monitoring and review of the process. Many schools have found that a review panel of staff can be an effective means of evaluating the process.

Governing bodies will need to have reports on aggregated targets and consider these in relation to the school development and staff development plans.

It is expected that the DFE will require information from LEAs and grant-maintained schools to review progress made.

Further reading

The Education (School Teacher Appraisal) Regulations 1991, HMSO.
Goddard, I and Emerson, C (1992) *Appraisal and your School*, Heinemann.
Burnell, S (ed) (1987) *Teacher Appraisal in Practice*, Heinemann.
Dilley, B (1989) *Appraisal and Appraisal Interviewing* Industrial Society Management in Education Series.

Managing Staff Development

Margaret Nicholls

Introduction

Definitions of staff development vary enormously. The best so far appears to be 'the sum total of formal and informal learning experiences throughout a person's career from initial training to retirement'.[1]

However, in managing these experiences positively there are several issues which must be addressed early on.

Climate

Much of the best professional development appears to happen by osmosis. Where the mangement of a school has created a receptive climate, where the staff are involved in the planning and decision-making, and where everyone – teaching and non-teaching staff alike – has access to quality training opportunities, then colleagues' enthusiasm and inspiration transmits itself to others and becomes a significant motivating factor.

Motivation

The factors that motivate colleagues to become actively involved in planned professional development are many and varied. One may be seeking promotion, another may perceive a gap in his or her own personal performance, yet another may strive to emulate a colleague or a friend. Frequently the perceptions are linked to either self-assessment or professional appreciation, often of a more senior colleague. Appraisal, sensitively handled and imaginatively organised, may also be a key motivating factor.

The creation of open working groups, either within departments or faculties or across the whole staff, where colleagues feel at ease and confident, with a clear working brief, is an effective way to identify both group and individual needs. It is also an excellent means of stimulating commitment.

Access

Consultants proliferate. Institutions are swamped with invitations for workshops, seminars, conferences and training opportunities.

But how do *staff* access the information and participate in the decision-making? How can they arrange release from teaching commitments, and acquire support for participation in the training (information technology/reprographics etc)?

These opportunities must be made accessible. Attention to detail in terms of involving colleagues will make the difference between successful positive experiences and dull, demotivating ones.

Key personnel must be easily identifiable and accessible. Right of access to the head for personal consultation should be expected and demanded. Senior staff should have responsibility for staff development written into their job decriptions. Formal inset groups responsible for co-ordination and management can be very helpful in terms of planning, information sharing and day-to-day running, as well as providing the mechanism by which staff development is matched to the school's development plan. Membership should be open and debate free, and all staff should feel they have access to information and the power to influence planning cycles.

How easy is this?

- Information/display area: Attractive? Accessible?
- Cover arrangements: Simple? Streamlined?
- Financial support: Swift? Simple? Immediately accessible?
- Feedback arrangements: Non-threatening? Productive?

Organisation

There are many possible models of organisation but all have common factors – how/when/where/who? – and if we wish to be successful we will not ignore them.

The school development plan

It is essential that all staff are aware of this and have access to it. The most critical features will obviously be the overall aims and objectives of the institution. The next issue will be aspects of the plan which impinge on departmental or individual staff, work and development.

To be effective, training and development opportunities should be set in the context of the development plan. This will assist with criteria for prioritising planning, selection and evaluation.

Using questionnaires

Initially, it is helpful to have an analysis of colleagues' perceptions of their own needs, priorities and capacities. Key staff (eg assistant teacher, head of department, head of year/house, senior teacher, deputy head, administrative colleague) can profitably work together to assist the whole staff in developing a questionnaire or review sheet that the in-service group can analyse before beginning to plan a year's in-service programme.

Balance needs

Alongside this, it is essential to review the aims and objectives of the institution to enable the management of the school to prioritise the needs which will inevitably be expressed. A balance has to be maintained between in-service training opportunities which benefit students and those which will personally reward individual members of staff.

Feedback and review

There needs to be a forum for reviewing who should go on what courses and how dissemination of the information and insight gained may be achieved in return. Naturally, this needs to be linked to the information already culled about priorities and both school and personal needs. It is then essential that someone within the institution (and preferably more than just the head) has an overview of the whole pattern.

This implies tight organisation, good record-keeping and easy access for all involved.

Content

Staff development falls into two main areas:

1. In-house needs

An institution may identify a specific need within its own staff for a particular expertise. Current examples include the need for support for those responsible for work that is failing within the parameters of the Children Act; legislation on school attendance; and procedures for dealing with child protection issues.

It may be that specific curriculum areas need attention, eg developments in Key Stage Three Technology; assessment techniques in Science; or support for language teachers offering their second or third languages within modern languages for all.

Needs identified in these areas may point towards the most appropriate providers with little opportunity for choice, however, it is well worth co-ordinators checking out providers from the point of view of appropriateness and value for money.

2. Needs presenting from externally imposed factors: Appraisal and professional review

The management of this is critical to its success or otherwise. Some education authorities and indeed some institutions see this as an integral part of proper professional development for staff. Observation of initial attempts would appear to show evidence that where this is the case appraisal is seen as non-threatening, creative and a support tool at all levels.

Detailed analysis of individual schemes would be inappropriate here, but these management guidelines will be useful:

• set the scene for all staff;

• even where institutions wish to avoid 'top down' delivery, it is helpful if key staff who will be reviewing others go through the process themselves first so that heads and deputies will inevitably be guinea pigs;

• attention given to proper job descriptions and personnel specifications for staff on appointment will save time, energy and frustration later;

• regular reviews and updates of job descriptions are essential;

• the setting of key tasks against school and departmental/ pastoral priorities at least each year and preferably termly, is also essential;

• create regular opportunities for all groups of staff to review and evaluate their work against both school and section priorities.

Finance

Budgetary considerations have a vital part to play in ensuring that staff are satisfied with any proposals for professional development. With the advent of LMS, more open access to school financial policies often brings added advantages. Value for money has to be demonstrated – how else can expenditure be justified? It is the clear responsibility of the head, together with the governors, in reviewing the allocation of resources, to set aside an appropriate sum to be devoted exclusively to in-service training/professional development. The whole staff should be aware of the mechanics of this exercise. Given the fact that neither training opportunities nor staff demand rarely arrive regularly, the more flexible a budget can be, the better. It is essential that those responsible for allocating resources retain a contingency fund to enable them to seize opportunities when they present themselves.

Sponsorship

There is rarely sufficient money to cover every eventuality. When planning training sessions which are either institution-led or -based, it is wise to investigate sponsorship in one form or another, eg from local hotels and catering organisations for venues and provisions, and from local industry and commerce for expertise, facilities and consumable resources. Educational charities too are often a source of funds, particularly for sponsorship of individual professional development.

It is well worth the investment of one person's time within the in-service group, the finance group, or the school as a whole, to check out all the possible alternative sources of finance.

Prime considerations

Finally, what are the most important issues to address when considering professional development for colleagues? Surely the most important has to be adequate provision, followed by right of access. Every colleague from the newly qualified teacher to the most senior member of staff heading for retirement is entitled to support and development at whatever level he or she feels is appropriate at the time.

Information and communication throughout the institution are vital. Institutions that flourish in all areas are those where equal support is given to their non-teaching staff. The quality of response given by dining-room assistants, by caretaking and services staff, not to mention administrative, secretarial and technician staff, is mirrored by quality provision for the students.

Proper participative planning and whole-school review and evaluation will enable everyone to feel that their professional development opportunities are one of the most valuable features of their professional lives.

KEY ISSUES

- Establish the needs of **all** staff.

- Ensure ownership by wide consultation.

- Embed the policy in the school development plan.

- Ensure sensitive handling of non-teaching staff and provide relevant, appropriate agendas carefully linked to whole-school policy.

- Evaluate information and communication systems and adjust as appropriate.

Further reading

Brighouse, T *What Makes a Good School?*, Teaching and Learning Series, Network Educational Press.

Donnelly, J (1991) *Managing Inset* Secondary Heads' Association (£3.50).

The Staff Development Manual Framework Press.

Bunnell S, *Teacher Appraisal in Practice* Heinemann.

The Industrial Society *In the Light of Torches*, Teacher Appraisal Suffolk Education Department.

References

1   Green H, National Educational Assessment Centre, Oxford.

Opportunities for Management Development for Teachers

Ron Glatter

All teachers are managers. Their conditions of employment recognise this by including both managerial and administrative tasks within the specification of 'professional duties' (DFE, 1993). The School Teacher's Review Body (1992) has said that, if we are to benefit from the increased devolution to schools, 'all teachers will need a range of management skills', and has urged Local Education Authorities (LEAs) and governing bodies to ensure that suitable opportunities for teachers to develop these skills are provided. Management and related activities are being assessed in the new inspection arrangements for schools (OFSTED, 1993).

What is management development?

Management development is that part of staff development which deals with the planned improvement of the managerial capabilities of individuals and groups. Many of the same principles apply as with staff development in general. The ultimate purpose is to enhance pupil's educational experience and achievements.

Who is management development for?

This is an important question, and not as easy to answer as it may seem. At least four potential beneficiaries can be identified, apart from the pupils themselves:

MBA (Education) Programme

The world of education in the '90s is a dynamic and demanding place. For a manager to be effective in this environment, formal learning and a professional qualification are becoming essential.

The possession of an MBA degree is widely recognised as demonstrating a commitment to professionalism in management and a high standard of academic attainment. The MBA (Education) programme at the University of Nottingham has been designed specifically to meet the needs of today's practising educational manager and to prepare the manager of tomorrow. Run in parallel with the University's highly regarded MBA programme for managers in industry and commerce, the MBA (Education) has the following features:

- Modular programme, allowing part-time study at a speed which meets the needs of the individual
- Teaching delivered in short residential blocks during Easter and Summer vacations
- Work-based assignments and directed study relate learning to the participant's institution
- Continuous assessment links theory with the application of skill and knowledge.

Entry into the programme takes place in April and August each year. Further details and application forms are available from:

**The Course Secretary, MBA (Education),
School of Management & Finance, Portland Building,
University of Nottingham, University Park,
NOTTINGHAM NG7 2RD
Telephone: Nottingham (0602) 515504
Fax: Nottingham (0602) 515503**

- *the individual teacher*, who, it can be argued, should have an entitlement to management development as a part of his or her career and personal development;

- *the school*, to help it become more effective in general through being well-managed;

- *the national system*, which needs a supply of staff who have received appropriate preparation for senior and middle management positions; and

- *the teaching profession*, since effective management development should enhance standards of professional performance.

Who should provide management development?

A lively debate has been raging recently about the respective roles of the school and other agencies. The Government-appointed School Management Tast Force, which operated from 1988 to 1992, emphasised the central role of the school. However its leader, David Styan, has warned of the danger of making too literal an interpretation of the term 'school-based' development, since this may lead us only to 'the parochial and mundane' (Styan, 1992). He argued that 'To achieve quality schooling and management development, responsibility must not be so diffuse as to leave everyone to leave it to someone else.'

If management development is to serve all the beneficiaries mentioned above, and if the requirements of the future as well as the present are to be met, then partnerships are needed between schools and a variety of other agencies.

The school and management development

Some recent developments, such as increased school autonomy and school development plans, emphasise the individual school and its immediate pupils as beneficiaries. Others, such as staff appraisal, put the emphasis more on the individual member of staff and her/his longer-term professional development. Schools need to balance these different emphases.

An important part of management development concerns the way the school organises its 'job-embedded' arrangements, what Bolam (1991) calls 'management support' as distinct from management education and training. This includes things like:

- job descriptions (to provide jobs that are manageable and stimulating);

- job enhancement and rotation;

- promotion and career development; and

- on-the-job assistance and coaching.

There are a number of ways that schools can provide direct support for management development in school. These include shadowing, mutual support groups and team-building. Wallace (1991) sets out the various possibilities. It is important that these are not seen as separate, disconnected activities but as part of a broader approach or plan to enhance overall managerial capability. This is easier said than done, and is likely to be more difficult the smaller the school is.

Increasingly, funds for management development are being devolved directly to school level. These funds will often be used to obtain external support for various kinds, for example from the LEA or from a consultant, or to make use of external course provision. The deployment of these funds should again form part of an overall approach, bearing in mind the four beneficiaries of management development indicated earlier, and the need to provide for more than just short-term requirements.

Forms of external support

There is now a huge and bewildering array of types of external support and of providers. Quality is variable – it is unequally distributed around the country and there is virtually no coordination. Much of it is too expensive for many schools to contemplate, particularly smaller ones or those with reducing rolls.

There are some ways of mitigating these problems. One is to combine into client-clusters: to quote David Styan (1992) again, '. . . unless schools cluster or combine in some way, they have little chance to commission the market to provide what is needed'.

Course (and consultancy services) are offered by a wide range of bodies including universities, professional associations, LEAs and private consultancy firms. Some industrial giants have also made places on their own management programmes available to staff from the education service.

Courses may be one- or two-day awareness-raising events, or substantial programmes leading to a diploma or master's degree. Management development is about much more than going on courses, which are often criticised for their lack of connection to participants' working situations, and also because they are generally attended by individuals from different schools who find it hard to implement the new ideas without support on returning to school. However, this is rapidly becoming an out-dated view because:

- longer courses are now mostly attended on a part-time basis, increasing the possibilities for a close relationship with the working context;

- courses often include substantial elements of project and enquiry work explicitly designed to link the course content to the school setting; and

- there are increasing facilities for groups of colleagues to follow a course together (for example, through the Open University's study group booking scheme).

Longer courses provide for the systematic development of understanding and reflection on practice, together with the scope for accreditation. However, it is important to realise that educational management involves a range of specialisms. Let us consider just some of the major areas which are relevant to the self-managing school:

- information technology applications;

- human resource management;

- personal effectiveness;

- curricular planning;

- financial management;

- marketing; and

- institutional development and evaluation.

It is clear that one- or two-person operations can hardly claim to be able to cover the full gamut without risking the charge of amateurism. We need a range of strong inter-disciplinary centres to give support to schools, as well as to individuals and LEAs, to help them to operate successfully under the new arrangements. We need a national strategy to strengthen the support systems and to secure co-ordinated provision of consistently high quality.

Distance learning

This has attracted growing interest in relation to educational management development. It can offer a number of advantages, including:

- flexibility in learning times and places for hard-pressed school staff;

- direct support to school-focused action learning through collaborative project work, etc;

- consistent standards and control of quality;

- effective and efficient use of scarce specialist expertise; and

- facilitation of access, especially in poorly-served or more 'remote' areas.

The School Management Task Force gave strong support to distance learning and related approaches as a way of bringing management development closer to the school and helping to make it more widely available at a realistic cost. The Open University has had nearly 20 years' experience of offering multi-media courses in educational management, and currently has an extensive programme of linked courses and modules. A number of other providers now have distance learning components, sometimes as modules alongside other modules which are taught conventionally.

Networks

These provide a means of creating more informal linkages with peers from different schools. Networks can be organised by schools themselves, but they often arise through membership of other bodies such as professional associations. They enable the exchange of experience, support and advice. A rather specific example of this kind of 'peer support' is the headship mentoring scheme initiated by the Task Force which was given some funding by the Government.

One network which is particularly relevant to management development is the British Educational Management and Administration Society (BEMAS). This provides a forum for all who are interested, whether in schools, colleges, universities or elsewhere, to come together for meetings and conferences and to receive publications. There are regional groups in most parts of the country. Workshops are offered on 'hot' topics such as management competences and total quality management.

Competences

A heated debate is in progress about how valid and helpful it is to specify school managers' work in terms of defined competences, and if so which model of competences to use. Advocates say they are valuable in providing a common framework for management development, assessment and accreditation. Sceptics claim that they encourage a mechanical approach and downplay the creative and holistic aspects of managing.

Esp (1993) provides a useful survey and discussion of a variety of approaches and pilot projects.

Conclusion

In the new climate of devolved funding for INSET, schools will have to make difficult and far-reaching decisions about management development for teachers. It is to be hoped that in making these judgements they will have regard to *all* the beneficiaries of the process, and that they will bear in mind one relatively uncontroversial passage from the White Paper 'Choice and Diversity' (DFE, 1992, paragraph 1.35): 'Most people are not born managers. The skills of management have to be learned and practised'.

References

Bolam, R (1991) 'Management and the quality of schooling: some implications of research and experience in England and Wales' in Ribbins, P, Glatter, R, Simkins, T and Watson, L (eds), *Developing Educational Leaders*, Longman in association with BEMAS.

DFE (1992) *Choice and Diversity: a new framework for schools*, Cm 2021, HMSO.

DFE (1993) *School Teachers' Pay and Conditions Document 1993*, HMSO.

Esp, D (1993) *Competences for School Managers*, Kogan Page.

OFSTED (1993) *Framework for the Inspection of Schools*, Office for Standards in Education.

The School Teachers' Review Body First Report 1992, Cm 1806, HMSO.

Styan, D (1992) 'School Management Task Force: review and reflection', *Management in Education*, Vol 6, No 3.

Wallace, M (1991) *School-Centred Management Training*, Paul Chapman Publishing.

4.8

Non-teaching Support Staff

Michael Warrington

Introduction

Local Management of Schools (LMS) has empowered schools to make decisions about their resource needs in a way previously not possible. The effect of this has been largely beneficial for schools, summarised in that very European word 'subsidiarity'! With the freedom to commit money to the development of previously underfunded areas, many headteachers have given a degree of priority to analysing their support staffing needs. There has been a consequent growth in the numbers of support staff and an increase in their level of remuneration.

Most local education authorities (LEAs) had rough-and-ready formulae for determining the number of clerks and technicians any school might have. The resulting numbers were rarely adequate. A recent survey for the Secondary Heads Association[1] showed wide variations in the non-teaching staff provision, not only between schools of different types, but also between schools of the same type (eg 11–16; 11–18, GMS, etc) in different areas of the country.

The 1986, 1988, 1991 and 1993 Education Acts have all created new problems and much administrative work for schools. (The 1993 Act is particularly huge.) At the same time the freedom conferred by LMS has enabled creative solutions to be tried. In the area of support for the curriculum, and hard-pressed teachers trying to 'deliver' it, this has meant new non-teaching roles and the breakdown of boundaries between the professional teacher and the non-teaching assistant. An increasing burden of administration falls on schools as the role of the LEA diminishes. A recently published report by Professor Peter Mortimore and associates for the DFE[2] contains a number of interesting case studies, which indicate the range of ideas around.

Inspection, Ofsted style, is having two effects on schools. First, it is creating a considerable amount of paperwork for schools, as they must assemble the documentary evidence and complete the many forms of information required by the inspectors. Second, the management of support staff is itself subject to inspection, requiring schools to take a careful look at an aspect of the school enterprise which has hitherto been seen as of lower priority than most other school matters.

Curriculum support

Good support can make an enormous difference to the quality of teaching and learning. It can be provided in a number of ways. For instance, there may be:

1. Staff who do all the school printing and copying work, prepare worksheets using desktop publishing programmes on computers, and provide IT support to pupils (and staff) in the classroom;

2. Librarians, not only supporting the curriculum through the medium of books, but also helping students use interactive video techniques, access data banks using CD ROMS or use modems for national networks;[3]

3. Technicians who support design, technology, home economics and science; and

4. Staff supporting the work of the English, Humanities, Languages and Maths faculties, which traditionally have had no such help.

Once teachers learn to use support staff effectively, which cannot be assumed to happen without conscious and active encouragement, they can concentrate on what they do best, which is teaching and learning in the classroom.

The school office

The days when that paragon of virtue, the school clerk, could cope with the entire needs of the staff and pupils, not to mention the eccentricities of the head, are gone. The volume of administrative work in schools has increased enormously in recent years. LMS itself has added a whole new layer of tasks. Under-provision in the school office creates unacceptable pressures on overworked support staff. It may also result in poor impressions being conveyed to visitors, who may alight on apparent chaos when they arrive for an appointment. No school can afford to have a poor reputation in this or any other area nowadays.

Management issues

Support staff account for about 4–6 per cent of the budget. Therefore it is wise to analyse very carefully what the needs of the school are in order to achieve cost-effectiveness. Almost always when schools start on this exercise they find that there is a considerable shortfall of provision. Quite often the strengths are in the wrong place, and staff in established roles may not have the skills now needed there. Significant resource and personnel management problems may well be revealed which can only be solved over a period of time. As always, it is sensible to involve the staff affected by the analysis, or at the very least to keep them fully informed. The changes which may be needed later will be much more easily accomplished if the staff see the need, understand the opportunities for themselves and do not feel threatened.

Effective management at this stage will involve a number of steps:

- creation of a long-term strategy;

- review of present provision – analysis of the work of each person;

- devising of a staffing structure with clear line management;

- revision and rewriting of job descriptions;

- grading and rewarding jobs on a rational basis within budget parameters; and

- fitting staff to jobs (and sometimes jobs to staff).

The working environment of support staff should be as much a matter of concern as that of teachers and pupils. This will involve careful scrutiny of:

- conditions of working – clear line management, task definition, training opportunities;

- the office environment – space, heating, lighting, air-conditioning, noise and interruption levels;
- the tools for the job; and
- use of new technology – word processors, training opportunities in new skills.

The rest of this article deals in a little more detail with factors involved in the effective management of support staff.

Getting rid of Topsy

The support staff in many schools would be hard-pressed to write down their job descriptions. Their jobs have grown like Topsy and they have been thoroughly taken advantage of, being asked to do far more than their inadequate pay merits. To put this right a number of steps are required:

1. Review the present provision – get the support staff to write down the tasks they do, who they do them for, and who they think is their line manager; analyse for overlap of function, inappropriate roles, anomalous situations.

2. Review need – ask support staff what the stress points are, what tasks they are doing which they feel either unqualified to do or unable to do due to time constraints; ask teaching staff at all levels what tasks they are doing that could be done by a trained non-teacher, and what would most help them to concentrate on their teaching role more effectively.

3. Review the support staffing structure, or create one – clarify the line management.

   Note: This may be the moment to make a major decision (with the governors) regarding whether or not to employ a more highly skilled and well-paid Bursar to run this side of the school staffing, as well as take responsibility for a range of other duties (eg repairs and maintenance, tendering for contracts, financial management). This decision has implications for the teaching staff. It may only be possible to make such an appointment by sacrificing a deputy head or senior teacher to pay for the post.

4. Draw up job descriptions as precisely as possible, indicating the line management.

5. Attach salary levels to jobs. Take advice from the LEA, which will have a well worked-out salary structure, at least on the

clerical side, and from the unions. Consult and get agreement with your own staff.

6. Internally advertise and interview for all posts in a way agreed in advance with the staff, so that they know what is happening. You might start with the highest paid posts and work down.

Costs

Almost inevitably this exercise will result in higher support staffing costs. It would be wise to calculate the likely cost before getting too far down the road. Budgetary constraints may prevent the full implementation of the plan, and there is then no point in raising false hopes.

Use national pay scales with local weightings. It is wise to stick to these, and unwise to start paying arbitrary salaries however imaginatively devised, which may be financially embarrassing after a while, and may also cause difficulties in neighbouring schools when their staff get to know what is being paid.

Calculation of annual costs can be complicated, especially for part-time posts. Holiday entitlement, which varies with length of service, must be taken into account. The LEA can help with this in the case of maintained schools.

A place fit for purpose – and for human beings

Many school offices are like Clapham Junction; a lot of traffic passes through them, and some of it could be re-routed elsewhere to relieve congestion. As in almost every other area of education, there has been a great expansion in the amount of work that support staff are asked to do. They cannot work efficiently with the stream of unwarranted interruptions, nor with staff coming in to borrow the stapler or to exchange gossip. It is in the interests of the institution to provide reasonable conditions of work, and your employees have a right to them for the sake of their health and sanity. Some of the questions a headteacher may wish to ask are:

• Are the lighting, heating and ventilation adequate?

• Do support staff have reasonable working spaces?

• Are the total clerical hours sufficient to get the work done without overburdening anyone?

- Are reception and telephones, which can be distracting, in a separate office?
- Is the switchboard adequate, with sufficient extensions to reach all areas of the school?
- Is the office equipped with modern technology: photocopier, fax machine, word processors, and other aids to good office practice?

The answers to these questions will be significant. They signal the value you place on the work of the support staff.

If the answer to any of them is negative, then perhaps consideration should be given to the production of an office development programme as part of the school development plan.

Similar questions may be asked to the library assistant, curriculum support staff, laboratory and design technicians and the IT technician, if there is one.

Most schools nowadays integrate the support staff fully, so that they share all facilities with the teaching staff. Some questions to ask here are:

- Are support staff given access to the staff room and its facilities?
- Do they have representation on the governing body?
- Are they consulted about matters in which they have an interest, eg a whole-school no smoking policy?
- Do support staff have regular meetings so that they have opportunities to express their views on matters of importance to them?

Support staff development

It can be argued that since the support staff are an essential part of the whole enterprise, they should therefore have regular appraisal like the teaching staff. In the same way, they should have training opportunities for their personal and professional development. Money should be earmarked in the budget to support this.

How much better it is if there is a climate in which support staff feel valued and have a desire for self-improvement and increased expertise. Morale, commitment and service to the school tend to increase in such circumstances.

Ofsted Inspection

If governors and heads are providing adequate resources and a pleasant environment for support staff to work in, if they are paying a decent rate for the job being asked, if they are responsive to the needs of staff and provide developmental opportunities, and if the staff have the skills they need to do the job, then they have nothing to fear when the inspectors descend on the school. If they are not doing these things, and if support staff are not being deployed effectively and efficiently, then they can expect criticism.

The *Framework for Inspection*[4] deserves careful scrutiny for references to support staff. Some of the references are to classroom assistants or the support of SEN or ESL staff, but there are clear references to other kinds of support staff.

You should ensure amongst other things that:

1. all your support staff have up-to-date job descriptions;

2. the level of support can be stated in appropriate terms in the following categories:

    *   general secretarial and office staff

    *   staff to support school finance systems

    *   technicians to support work in practical subjects

    *   librarians, medical staff

    *   non-teaching classroom support and its distribution across curricular areas

In part 8, *Headteacher's Forms*, form 20 requires information about support staff.

Finally, what answers can you give to these questions?:

*   How thoroughly do your support staff understand the implications of their job descriptions?

*   How far are they motivated by the responsibilities delegated to them?

*   To what extent are non-teaching staff drawn into the overall work of the school?

*   To what extent is the efficiency of teachers and the effectiveness of teaching affected by non-teaching staff provision?

*   Is there sufficient non-teaching support to ensure effective day-to-day running of the school?

*   When did the school last conduct an audit of its staffing requirements?

You may be asked, so be prepared!

References

1 Warrington, M (1992) *Managing Non Teaching Staff*, SHA.
2 Mortimore, Peter et al (November 1992) *The Innovative Uses of Non-Teaching Staff in Primary and Secondary Schools*, Institute of Education.
3 *Model Specification for a School Library* (1990) The Library Association.
4 *The Handbook for the Inspection of Schools*, Part 2, Ofsted.

4.9

Improving Management Performance: Can Competence-based Approaches Help?

Peter Earley

School management is essentially about working with and through other people, creating the conditions which enable both pupils *and* teachers to achieve effective learning. It is only recently, however, that there has been a proper recognition that a school's most important resource is its staff and that 'investing in people' is an effective route to school improvement. What are the best ways of developing people or managing a school's human resources is, of course, more problematic, although the School Management Task Force (SMTF) report *The Way Forward* makes a number of helpful suggestions in relation to the development of school managers. It suggests, for example, that we need to reorientate our focus and give emphasis to such matters as:

- support for self-directed study by individuals, school teams, peer groups;

- in-school and near-to-the-school training;

- flexitime study;

- distance learning materials, information packs and projects;

- school-determined agenda; and

- performance enhancement.

What are competences?

One approach to management development that meets many of the SMTF's recommendations is that associated with 'competences'. The notion of competence has now become increasingly used in education and I don't just mean as a term of abuse! (The terms 'incompetence' or 'merely competent' are never used by advocates of this approach to development.) Efforts are currently being made, for example, to improve the links between initial teacher training, the induction of newly-qualified teachers and INSET during the early years of teachers' careers through the development of profiling and competence-based approaches to professional development. However, although the term has become more commonplace – dare one say even accepted? – it has tended to be defined in different ways. Many commentators use the term broadly to include knowledge, skills, values and attitudes, whilst others attach to it a much more specific meaning.

In the arena of management development and training, competences have tended to be defined either in terms of:

- the characteristics of effective or 'superior' managers, or

- the actual performance required of managers.

The former definition, derived from North America, gives much importance to the personal competences that individuals bring with them to the job and sees competence as 'the predisposition to behave in ways associated with the achievement of successful performance'. The latter definition stresses outcomes and 'the ability to perform work activities to the *standards* required in employment'. This approach to competence, which underpins the national system of vocational qualifications (NVQs) in England and Wales, does not deny that qualities, skills and knowledge are needed but states that it is first necessary to decide what competent management performance would constitute. Management standards centre on the requirements of the managerial role to be performed rather than on individual managers and the attributes they should possess. Standards attempt to provide specifications or benchmarks against which the performance of individual managers or management teams can be assessed. Performance criteria define explicitly what is expected of effective performance at work. It is probably most helpful to see the two approaches as complementary, with each one giving different emphases to 'personal' or 'functional' competences. Most importantly, both approaches see learning starting from the needs and requirements of the learner and the organisation in which they work.

How can competences be used by schools?

Competence-based approaches to mangement development are becoming increasingly common in schools, especially in relation to profiling, assessment and development centres, and individual manager certification. The latter has largely been initiated by the Management Charter Initiative (MCI) and its attempt to devise a set of generic standards for managers which form the basis of an NVQ. Before considering the value of these approaches it is worth briefly describing the types of competences that have been identified and how they can be used by schools. The examples in Tables 4.9.1 and 4.9.2 may help.

The main thrust of the work of assessment centres is towards the development of senior staff – usually heads and prospective heads – although the process has been adapted to help inform selection and appointment procedures. To date, the MCI standards have been mainly used for the purposes of accreditation and certification although using competence-statements to underpin qualifications is only one of a number of their possible uses.

Using competences in schools

Competence-statements or standards can be used in a number of ways (Earley, 1992):

- as a self-reflective and self-assessment tool
- as part of the appraisal process
- providing goals for learners and defining learning objectives
- as criteria for selection for jobs, education or training
- for the development of management qualifications
- for school review and institutional development
- as the basis of job descriptions
- for the design of development and training programmes.

Although there are a growing number of local education authorities (LEAs) and schools making use of the MCI competences (eg see Jagger, 1991; Whitson, 1992), there has been considerable debate about the relative value of *generic* competences as opposed to those which relate more specifically to the world of schools. School

School management competences	NEAC added 4 new competences in 1993:
Administrative competences 1. Problem analysis 2. Judgement 3. Organisational ability 4. Decisiveness **Interpersonal competences** 5. Leadership 6. Sensitivity 7. Stress tolerance **Communicative competences** 8. Oral communication 9. Written communication **Personal breadth competences** 10. Range of interest 11. Personal motivation 12. Educational values	• Divergent thinking/ creative problem-solving • Developmental orientation • Boundary management • Pedagogic leadership These will be integrated with the existing list of 12 as new materials are produced for the extension phase. (Green, 1992)

An assessment or development centre identifies key competences, designs task-related exercises to test them, trains assessors to observe the performance of participants on the exercises and produces a personal report about each participant. The process takes about one and a half days with a further two or three days spent by assessors reaching a 'consensus' on a participant's performance. The final report focuses on the above 12 competences with a section on strengths followed by suggestions relating to improvement and further professional development. A feedback interview is offered to each participant and the outline of a professional development plan agreed with links to an appropriate mentor. (Green, 1991.)

Table 4.9.1 *Example 1: National Educational Assessment Centre*

Management South (SMS), a consortium of 14 LEAs in south-east England, has produced and trialled a set of school management standards which attempt to refine and extend the work of MCI. Using a similar approach and methodology, four key roles or functions have been identified:

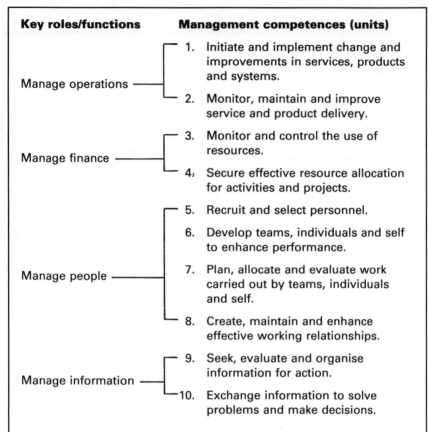

Key roles/functions	Management competences (units)
Manage operations	1. Initiate and implement change and improvements in services, products and systems.
	2. Monitor, maintain and improve service and product delivery.
Manage finance	3. Monitor and control the use of resources.
	4. Secure effective resource allocation for activities and projects.
Manage people	5. Recruit and select personnel.
	6. Develop teams, individuals and self to enhance performance.
	7. Plan, allocate and evaluate work carried out by teams, individuals and self.
	8. Create, maintain and enhance effective working relationships.
Manage information	9. Seek, evaluate and organise information for action.
	10. Exchange information to solve problems and make decisions.

The above generic management competences have been derived through a process of analysing manager's jobs and breaking them down into their component parts. Each unit of competence is subdivided into elements which consist of performance criteria against which individuals (or teams) must provide *evidence* of competence which is then assessed. The onus for collecting evidence is on the individual (or team), usually with the assistance of a mentor. Assessment of achievement against the national management standards is sought by gathering evidence of performance, usually by means of a portfolio, under the pressure of real work. Four basic sources of evidence can be used: workplace performance, historical evidence, performance on specially set tasks (as for example in an assessment centre) and less direct evidence through questioning. The dominant source of evidence tends to be performance at work; where possible, evidence should be produced in the course of the normal outcomes of work. Assessment, by trained assessors, is the process of obtaining and judging evidence against the performance criteria. (Day, 1990.)

Table 4.9.2 *Example 2: Management Charter Initiative*

- the management of policy
- the management of learning
- the mangement of people
- the management of resources.

(The school management standards and an evaluation of their use in schools is available from School Management South or NFER.)

Perhaps more importantly, there now exists sufficient empirical evidence about the use of competences for school management development – be they sector-specific, generic, personal or functional competences – for some conclusions to be drawn (Earley, 1993). A growing number of Schools and LEAs are using the SMS competences for self-appraisal and school review and three Universities are currently offering School Management qualifications based on the SMS key roles.

Are competence-based approaches worth considering?

The simple answer to the above question is 'yes', although the success of competence-based approaches to training and development depends on a number of key factors, all of which will be found to varying degrees in schools. Success is most likely to depend upon the following:

- the quality of the relationships between mentors and 'learners'
- the credibility and competence of the assessors
- the developmental culture or 'ethos' of the school
- the support of senior management
- the willingness to provide the necessary resources.

For many, a major advantage of this approach is that it emphasises workplace performance – generally recognized to be the most effective locus for management development – and that it necessitates establishing an infrastructure which encourages and enables manager and management development to occur. The use of the competences tends to be practitioner-driven, rather than being determined by the training provider, and allows for the better identification of training and development needs. Competences enable career or personal development planning to be given a higher profile, whilst also empowering and motivating individuals (and teams) to use the competences in ways which reflect their own needs and those of the schools in which they work. Most import-antly, unlike much of what is traditionally considered to be in-service education and training, such an approach is likely to impact directly on performance.

There is, of course, also a downside in using competences for development: some, for example, find the long list of behaviours or criteria demoralising, the language unappealing and the 'owner-ship' question difficult to resolve. It should be stressed that a comeptence-based approach is but one of a number of development strategies and it may be an approach that suits some individuals and schools more readily than others. What does seem to be the case, however, is that effective management performance of *all* those in management positions is generally seen as critical to a school's success. For some, working with competences has been found to be a powerful force for institutional and individual development, encouraging schools and their staff to consider the extent to which their systems and structures facilitate or hinder their development. If schools are to become 'learning organisations' – where development and training (of both pupils and adults) is of major concern – they can ill afford to ignore competence-based developments. As a headteacher involved in the SMS competences project remarked: if a criterion-referenced, outcomes-based assess-ment system using profiles and records of achievement 'is good enough for our pupils then who is to say it's not good enough for us?' He may have a point.

References

Day, M (1990) 'Management competences come out', *Competences & Assessment*, 13, pp 3–5.

Earley, P (1992) 'Using competences for school management develop-ment' *British Journal of In-Service Education*, Vol 18, No 3.

Earley, P (1993) 'Developing competence in schools: A critique of standards-based approaches to management development' *Educa-tional Management & Administration* (Vol 21, No 4.)

Green, H (1991) 'Assessment for senior management development', *Management in Education*, Vol 5, No 4, pp 35–38.

Green, H (1992) *The use of an assessment centre approach, a personnel competence model and mentoring for the development of head-teachers*. NEAC: Oxford Polytechnic.

Jagger, J (1991) 'Improving competence', *Managing Schools Today*, Vol 1, No 4, pp 34–39.

School Management Task Force (1990) *Developing School Manage-ment: The Way Forward*, HMSO, London.

Whitson, S (1992) 'Certified progress', *Education*, 25 September.

The National Standard of 'Investors in People'

Does it have a place in the Management of Schools?

Hazel Barker and Mike Bell

'Investors in People' (IIP) has been developed in response to business demand and endorsed by the Confederation of British Industry (CBI). The 'Investors In People' standard is based on the experience of many successful UK companies, who have all found that their performance has been improved by a planned approach to:

- setting and communicating organisational goals;

- developing their people to meet these goals; so that

- what people can do (and are motivated to do) matches what the organisation needs them to do.

Although designed primarily for the profit-motivated company, the factors itemised above are clearly fundamental to the effective management of schools, or for that matter, other educational institutions, because they provide a sound basis for continuous organisational improvement.

In essence, IIP is a key element in Total Quality Management (TQM) complementing other systems-based standards (eg BS 5750) by focusing upon the essential factor in every organisation – *people*.

If you are interested in discovering how near you are to the standard, ask yourself the following basic questions about your own school or college:

Y/N

- Do you have a business plan, with clearly identified goals and targets? ☐

- Could your people explain those goals and targets to a customer, client or new colleague? ☐

- Can they explain their job, and identify clearly its importance to the school/college and to whom they are responsible? ☐

- Do they know that there is commitment to developing everyone's skills and qualities? ☐

- Are they all – both teaching and support staff – aware of the opportunities that exist for their own development? ☐

- Do they experience the commitment of managers at all levels (including governors) in their everyday work? ☐

The response you gave to these questions will give you a rough guide of how committed your school/college is to investing in its people, what it has achieved so far and how much there is still to do. If you answered 'no' to all the questions, do not dismay.

Few of the organisations we are working with currently (whether in the public or private sector, or large or small, or service or manufacturing) meet the IIP standard in full. However, without exception, their senior managers have all reached the conclusion that investing in their people is one of the most effective ways of improving organisational performance, and have decided to do something about it. Interestingly, many of the schools and colleges we are advising are well on the way to achieving IIP status, and are in no way falling behind their business counterparts. Whether this is the result of recent legislation, the influence of governors with business acumen, more effective management development of key personnel within the institution, a combination of all three or just the way it has always been, I will leave you to decide. I have drawn my own conclusions.

Staff training and development

We have found that the process of working towards IIP provides the rigour which is frequently lacking within schools and colleges in terms of the cohesive development of staff – and I stress that this incorporates the development of support, as well as teaching staff.

Many institutions already have a written plan setting out their goals and targets for the next three to five years. However, few have considered how employees will contribute to achieving the plan and have not attempted to specify how staff development needs will be assessed and met. Fewer still will have attempted to communicate to all employees a vision of where the school/college is going – and, most importantly, the contribution employees will make to its success.

This is not easy, but the benefits are a resultant clarity of direction which could seldom be achieved otherwise. The process can also provide keen motivation for staff who are overloaded by the constant changes besetting them, and the poor press education often receives.

Additionally, IIP requires that strategic teams identify the resources for training and development in the corporate plan, and that anyone having managerial responsibility be capable of reviewing training and development needs regularly with each employee. This negotiation is, preferably, to be addressed in the context of achieving objectives and setting targets and standards linked, as appropriate, to National Vocational Qualifications (NVQs) (eg Management Charter Initiative) and, in Scotland, Scottish Vocational Qualifications (SVQs). It goes without saying that it should be a positive and beneficial encounter for all. This may not be an easy task for many institutions. At its heart is the requirement to train all supervisors and managers to carry out the reviews effectively; and to communicate effectively to all employees the nature of the procedure, and its anticipated outcomes.

Furthermore, the IIP standard requires that action be focused within the organisation upon the training needs of all new recruits (at whatever level) and the continual development and improvement of skills of existing employees. This relates equally to the senior managers of the school or college.

Evaluation

Finally, to gain IIP, organisations are required to have a system for evaluating the effectiveness of any training and development undertaken, in the light of corporate performance. Once this review has been undertaken at top level, then training and development plans must be revised and new targets set. Those schools and colleges which already have clearly identified quality procedures will find it much easier to implement these changes. Where a quality manual exists, then it is a relatively simple procedure to extend the various sections to incorporate the IIP standards.

Inspection

Increasingly, IIP may be utilised as an aid to the now established four-year cycle of school inspection awarded to contractors by the Office for Standards in Education (OFSTED). *The Handbook for the Inspection of Schools* which is used by OFSTED Inspectors will oblige schools more than ever before to view their structure corporately. As this idea begins to take root in the state system it may well be that a cultural shift may ensue. The documentation which is required by OFSTED is considerable and will need to be viewed positively as a tool for school development.

The IIP process which is being pursued by many schools as a tool to assist with staff, and ultimately organisational development, may increasingly be seen in the context of external inspection, in that IIP required documentation has immediate relevance to documentation for external inspection. Furthermore, working towards IIP sets an organisational agenda for the medium term ie the period between external inspections. Finally, action planning required as part of an inspection derived strategy is closely paralleled by the requirements of the IIP process. 'Investors In People' can assist education organisations to respond to those challenges which currently abound in education.

Shift in culture

Undoubtedly, the recent legislative changes have required educational establishments to move towards a more market-orientated model, to a greater or lesser extent. This, in turn, has demanded new management skills of a more technical nature to be developed by senior staff and a commensurate change in attitude – and, ultimately behaviour – by all the people working within the organisation. This shift in culture can undoubtedly be aided, and therefore eased, by the systematic pursuit of IIP. Although it may not be possible to quantify and measure the precise impact upon the attitudes and commitment of people, which will inevitably be highly specific to each school or college, the benefits will be no less important than those which can be easily predicted.

With the current heightened emphasis upon public relations, the need for a skilled and motivated workforce is essential for the delivery of an education service which is seen to be effective. Being viewed by the outside world to be an IIP will thus bring benefits in an increasingly competitive and demanding environment where

survival can no longer be guaranteed. Clearly linked to establishing a good reputation for the institution is the concept of the satisfied customer. Satisfying customers undoubtedly goes further than simply assuring the quality of output. It is the organisation which places importance upon employees understanding the vision of where the organisation is going, and how they will contribute to its success, which gives credence to the glossy brochure, the press release and the speeches of the management at the various fora.

Certainly, IIP can give teeth to quality programmes because, undoubtedly, any commitment to the pursuit of quality by those at the top, can only be achieved by a commitment to involve and develop everyone to play their part. The goal of quality in any business, ie the cost-effective delivery of a service which consistently meets customer demands and expectations, must be understood and supported by people at every level – and in every function.

The challenges facing all of us in education require a fundamental change in our attitudes and actions. IIP is clearly the standard to aspire to for those schools and colleges who wish to respond to the challenges, and seize the opportunities which present themselves at the current time.

Further information about the 'Investors In People' initiative may be obtained from your local Training and Enterprise Councils (TECs). The details of the services available to you may vary slightly from TEC to TEC but all will range from free advice and practical materials to modestly-priced consultancy. Alternatively, for informal advice please do not hesitate to contact Hazel Barker, author of this article.

KOGAN PAGE

The Children Act and Schools
A Guide to Good Practice
Ben Whitney

" A well balanced and accurate analysis of the legislation... essential reading for teachers."
NASWE JOURNAL

Using case studies based on real situations, **Ben Whitney** highlights areas of the Act which are of special relevance within schools. He demonstrates how to gain the greatest possible advantage from the legislation, avoiding its potentially costly pitfalls, for the mutual benefit of everyone involved.
This comprehensive book examines the following issues in detail:

* *why children needed a new law*
* *child protection*
* *parental responsibility*
* *children's rights*
* *truancy and classroom behaviour.*

£12.95 Pbk   ISBN 0 7494 1115 5
160 pages **Published November 1993** order ref: KS115

Essential School Leadership
Developing Vision and Purpose in Management
Gary Holmes

"Outlines in five short chapters an agenda for reflection and action that is both convincing and challenging."
TES

"A little gem of a book... essential reading for head teachers."
EDUCATION

In this accessible survey of leadership challenges, **Gary Holmes** analyses the complex and often conflicting messages that confront today's school leaders and breaks them down to five essentials:

* *building vision and purpose* • *leading learning* • *managing people*
* *dilemmas, problems and purposes* • *accountability.*

Working from this five-point plan, using case studies, the author builds up a valuable model of leadership that balances the essential with the optional.

£14.95 Pbk ISBN 0 7494 0985 1   160 pages
Published November 1993 order ref: KS985

KOGAN
PAGE

Part Five

Curriculum Management

"Archimedes"
"Here Sir"
"Babbage"
"Sir"
"Curie"
"Yes Sir"
"Diesel"
"Here Sir"
"Einstein"
"Yes Sir"
"Faraday"
"Sir"

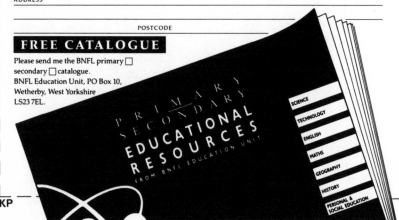

Managing the Curriculum

Barry Hilditch

Managing the curriculum since the 1988 Education Act has taken on a new meaning as the full impact of Local Management of Schools (LMS) and the National Curriculum has become clear to those responsible for running secondary schools. Only time will tell whether the primary aim of raising the standards has been achieved. What is already evident is that there is a better opportunity to plan ahead with important decisions being made at a local level and for resources, however limited, to be targeted at priorities identified within the school itself. There are concerns and indeed real problems in managing this monumental change, especially when revisions and changes are brought in before the whole of the National Curriculum has been put in place and the full extent of the impact of assessment on the curriculum felt.

Who controls the curriculum?

The responsibilities of the headteacher and the governing body are set out in legislation and in most schools now form the basis of a sound and fruitful working relationship between the school management team and the governing body, often through a curriculum sub-committee. Table 5.1.1 reminds us where responsibilities lie.

School management

The role of the senior management team is to ensure that the curriculum is well planned, changes are implemented and the delivery

---

Governing Body

Decides curriculum policy taking into account the National Curriculum, the LEA Curriculum Policy Statement and the views of the school and community.
Approves arrangements for sex education and RE.
Confirms the delivery of the curriculum and receives reports.
Decides the number of staff required to deliver the curriculum.

Headteacher

Proposes a detailed curriculum plan after consultation within the school which ensures delivery of the statutory elements.
Organises the delivery of the curriculum; monitors and reports.
Advises on number and skills of staff needed.

Table 5.1.1 *Division of responsibilities for the curriculum*

is monitored. The effective and efficient delivery of the curriculum is of ever increasing importance with the growth of direct competition between schools, the publication of league tables and a level of funding which is increasingly insufficient to meet the resource demands needed to give better opportunities for all our pupils.

Within the school's management structure, roles and responsibilities related to the planning and delivery of the curriculum must be established and known to all staff, who should also be aware of the process of consultation and decision-making with regard to curriculum matters. As schools increasingly come to take full advantage of the autonomy provided by LMS, to develop a working partnership with governors and to see the advantages of development planning, they have come to realise the need to establish planning cycles to cover all important annual aspects of the school's work. This process also brings a greater sense of order and structure to the whole process of management including the curriculum.

Key questions to be addressed

In addition to the exact composition and content of the curriculum, some basic issues need to be considered.

Timing and organisation of the school day

Look carefully at the present format and check:

* the length of the school day;

Task	Date	Action
Review current curriculum	Sept	Curriculum Group
Identify changes for next academic year. Relate to School Development Plan	Sept	Curriculum Group
Establish projected pupil numbers	Sept	Curriculum Deputy
Draft curriculum model and staffing predictions	Oct	Curriculum Deputy
Consultation and discussion	Oct/Nov	Management Group Curriculum Group
Identify possible changes to Governing Body sub-committee	Nov	Head/Curriculum Deputy
Agree curriculum model	Dec	Governing Body sub-committee
Detailed staffing requirements	Jan	Curriculum Deputy
Staffing establishment agreed	Feb	Governing Body sub-committee
Production of model timetable and identify subject areas for new staff	Feb	Curriculum Deputy
Approve staffing needs and check against budget	April	Governing Body sub-committee
Adverts and appointments	May/June	Governors
Timetable production	June	Curriculum Deputy
Establish forms and teaching groups	June	Heads of School Heads of Department
Final timetable and class lists	July	Curriculum Deputy

Note: Management and Curriculum Groups are staff consultative bodies.

Table 5.1.2 *A typical curriculum planning cycle*

- the amount of time pupils are actually taught compared to the total time for registration and collective worship;
- the relative length of morning and afternoon sessions;

- if the lessons are of equal length;
- if the timetable gives all subjects a fair distribution of morning and afternoon lessons as well as within the week.

Balance of time

With the increasing pressure of the demands of the full National Curriculum in the planning stages, and the desire for schools to retain areas like personal and social education and some subjects outside the National Curriculum, it is frequently found that the balance of time between the competing subjects is best addressed over the total length of the key stage and not year by year.

Key stage 3

Year	Mathematics	Science	English	Core Total	%
7	3	3	4	10	40
8	4	3	3	10	40
9	3	4	3	10	40
Total over key stage	10	10	10		

The core subjects contribute 10 of the 25 period week (40%) with each subject having 10 periods (13.33%) of the 3 year total of time.

Key stage 4

Year	Geography/ History	Modern Languages	Option 1	Option 2	Total
10	3	2	2	3	10
11	2	3	3	2	10

In key stage 4 GCSE courses cannot be delivered in two hours per week, but can be allocated more time by changing time allocations for years 10 and 11.

Table 5.1.3 *Balance of time for core subjects*

Course time

The increased pressures of covering the full National Curriculum and retaining even a limited amount outside these requirements may require taking a close look at the actual number of hours

available for the whole curriculum and the time available for each course costed out. With a pupil year of 190 days, 185 is a realistic number of days on which pupils will be effectively taught for, say, five hours per day. This would give 925 hours of tuition per year and 2775 for the three years covering key stage 3.

As there is a reduction in the number of days in year 11, it is probably at key stage 4 that curriculum managers will need to look most carefully, with many schools having to seriously consider short courses in order to retain viable option time which will allow subjects such as art, music, a second foreign language and a second humanity (history or geography or religious studies) to be offered.

The National Curriculum: September 1994

September 1994 represents a significant step in the National Curriculum: Key Stage 3 is completed, although a degree of uncertainty exists as a result of the Dearing review which promises a less content-laidened curriculum and possibly more flexibility at Key Stage 4.

	Key Stage 3			Key Stage 4	
	7	8	9	10	11
English	*	*	*	*	*
Science	*	*	*	*	*
Mathematics	*	*	*	*	*
Technology	*	*	*	*	*
Geography	*	*	*	*	
History	*	*	*	*	
Modern Languages	*	*	*		
Art	*	*	*		
Music	*	*	*		
PE	*	*	*		
Welsh	*	*	*	*	*

*NB:*Schools in Wales which did not previously teach Welsh will be two years behind.

Table 5.1.4 *The progress of National Curriculum Implementation; September 1994*

In Key Stage 3, all subjects should be on stream throughout the three years, 7, 8 and 9. By September 1994, more realistic tests should be given in the three core subjects, and content requirement may be reduced, particularly in the foundation subjects.

The uncertainty resulting from the review will be most felt in planning Key Stage 4. Difficulties concerning technology in 1993 will remain, along with strong feelings that the implementation of the requirements for geography or history should be delayed until the final outcome of the revision is known. The present require-ment, which will be kept for 1994 and 1995, requires that either geography or history should be studied as a full GCSE course or both as combined short courses. In 1995 modern foreign languages will be required as either a full or short course.

In managing the curriculum it is impossible to ignore many other aspects of school management which will need to be linked if the primary aim of the effective and efficient delivery of the curriculum is to be achieved. These will include:

- whole-school assessment policy;

- staff appraisal and development;

- budget management which ensures that the staffing and resource needs are clearly identified and then matched to expenditure; and

- non-teaching support staff.

The success of managing the curriculum will be reflected in the school's standing in the local community, staff morale and, above all, in the pupils themselves.

5.2

Special Needs

Dee Palmer-Jones

The 1993 Education Act has a number of implications for special needs, and sets out to secure that provision for special educational needs is consistent nationally, and that the time taken to provide statements for the small number of pupils who need them is much shorter than in the past.

One result of the Act is a 'Code of Practice on the Identification and Assessment of Special Education Needs', issued by the DFE in draft form in November 1993, to be implemented in September 1994. The Act and the Code of Practice have considerable implications for every school's management of special educational needs (SEN), the most significant being that:

- the needs of most pupils 'will be met in the mainstream, and without a statutory assessment or statement of special educational needs';

- the governing body of a school is now responsible for ensuring that provision is made for pupils with special educational needs and that it must 'closely monitor' the work of the school on behalf of pupils with SEN;

- every school must draw up a policy on SEN;

- every mainstream school should now have an SEN coordinator; and that

- time-limits will now be given, within which assessments and statements must be made by the LEA.

Definition of special needs

A child has a *special educational need* if he or she has a learning difficulty which calls for special education provision to be made for him or her.

A child has a *learning difficulty* if he or she:

1. has a significantly greater difficulty in learning than the majority of children of the same age;

2. has a disability which prevents or hinders the child from making use of the kind of education facilities provided for children of the same age in schools within the area of the LEA; or

3. is under five and falls within the definition of 1 or 2 above.

Special educational provision refers to that which is additional to, or different from, the provision made generally for others of the child's age in maintained schools in the area.

It is estimated that nationally about 20 per cent of children have SEN at some time, though only 2 per cent will require the LEA to determine provision.

Code of Practice

In November 1993 the DFE published the 'Draft Code of Practice on the Identification and Assessment of Special Educational Needs'. The following procedure is based on that code of practice, which is anticipated to be implemented in September 1994.

Stage 1:   The class or subject teachers identify a child's special educational needs, gather information and take initial action.

Stage 2:   The school's SEN coordinator takes lead responsibility for managing the child's special educational provision, working with the child's teachers.

Stage 3:   Teachers and the SEN coordinator are supported by specialists from outside the school.

Stage 4:   The LEA consider the need for a statutory assessment and, if necessary, make a multidisciplinary assessment.

Stage 5:   The LEA consider the need for a statement of SEN and if appropriate make a statement.

The first three stages are a continuous and systematic cycle of planning, intervention and review to enable the child with SEN to learn and progress. Few children will progress through all the stages, and the vast majority will be catered to within the first three stages, within school.

The within-school cycle

1. Identify pupils with special educational needs;
2. collect information and consult with parent and child;
3. assess the child's needs;
4. draw up a plan of action;
5. implement the plan and set a review date; and;
6. review progress.

Identification

The first expressions of concern may come from the teacher or from the parents. A formal school SEN audit is useful, in which data is collected from class or subject teachers, results of standardised assessments within school (eg reading/numeracy) and National Curriculum information.

Collecting information and consulting with parents and the child

Where a special need has been identified, detailed information should be collected from all who teach the child; the parents should be contacted and their perspective obtained and the child's perceptions should also be obtained.

Assessing the child's needs

Once the information is gathered and a full picture obtained, the child's precise needs should be assessed, and decisions made concerning how the needs can be best addressed.

Individual action plan

This should be written, and should state curricular needs, teaching requirements within the classroom, non-curricular needs, and the date when progress will be reviewed.

All teachers who are involved with the child should be informed of the action plan, and the strategies put into action.

Review

When the child's progress is reviewed, the parents should be involved. If the child is not making progress, the SEN coordinator should take the lead in investigating the child's learning difficulty further; the action plan should be re-written, and a further review date set.

If progress is still not satisfactory, then the head should consider referring the child to the LEA for statutory assessment. In order to do this, the school must have written information on: educational and other assessments; views of the parents and of the child; the child's health; and evidence of the school's intervention at all previous stages, including the individual plans and reviews, and the involvement of other professionals. Without such evidence it is unlikely that the LEA will consider statutory assessment.

The governing body

It is the responsibility of the governing body to:

• do its best to ensure that necessary provision is made for pupils with SEN;

• ensure that if a pupil has SEN, the needs are made known to all who teach him or her;

• ensure that teachers in school are aware of the importance of identifying and providing for SEN;

• draw up and report annually to parents on their policy for pupils with SEN; and

• ensure that pupils with SEN participate fully in the activities of the school.

Policy

The school's SEN policy must include:

1. Information about the school's SEN provision:
    –   the name of the SEN coordinator;

- admissions arrangements;
- SEN specialism and any special units; and
- any building adaptations and special facilities.

2. Information about the school's policies for identification, assessment and provision for all pupils with SEN:
   - the school's objective for pupils with SEN;
   - identification assessment, monitoring and review procedures;
   - use of any staged approach;
   - policy on access to the National Curriculum;
   - policy and priorities for the allocation of resources to pupils with SEN;
   - integration arrangements within the school; and
   - criteria for monitoring the success of the school's SEN policy.

3. Information about the school's staffing policies:
   - staff experience and qualifications;
   - school's SEN service training policy;
   - arrangements for partnership with parents;
   - use of external support services;
   - links with special schools; and
   - links with medical and social services.

Pupils with statements

The Code of Practice requires that statements are reviewed annually. It also emphasises that the annual review in the academic year two years before that in which the child reaches 16 is significant in preparing for his/her transition to the FE sector and adult life.

That annual review should therefore include a 'transition plan' [see paragraphs V1: 37–38].

5.3

Pupil Assessment

Roger Fetherston

Of all the activities teachers engage in, assessment, marking and recording pupils' work is probably the most essential and time-consuming of them all. The development of the National Curriculum has further raised the status of assessment by stating that it 'becomes an important influence on judgements about quality and performance'. (Croner 1992)

In the last 18 months we have witnessed enormous changes in the pattern of assessment and recording associated with the National Curriculum. From the excessively bureaucratic, audit-orientated model focused on the many hundreds of Statements of Attainment, we now operate in a 'slimmed down' world. National tests which were described as having 'an essential role to play in raising expectation, defining standards and providing secure information for parents about their children's progress' (DFE, The Government's Response to The Dearing Interim Report 1993) are now reduced in time and content. For seven year-olds there is to be a concentration on 'the basics'; for 14-year-olds only english, science and mathematics will be tested.

More significant are the changes to teacher assessment which effectively de-regulate them. Teachers now have the freedom to devise their own systems of assessment and record-keeping of classwork, whilst being faithful to the programmes of study. Such emancipation from the SOA style of record-keeping should lead to more enlightened and realistic measures of 'levelness', even though the very notion of the central pillars of ten progressive levels of achievement is now being seriously challenged.

Assessment Policy

While the National Curriculum sets a changing assessment pattern it is clear that in the context of the new school inspection framework, assessment figures highly. The Handbook for Inspection of Schools (1992) requires inspectors to consider the school assessment policy. In particular, inspectors will look at the quality of assessment, recording and reporting, and the management thereof.

Those who have a stake in the policy will extend beyond the staff and include governors (who should fully endorse the policy), parents and pupils. Involvement of these parties at appropriate times will bring obvious benefits. An example might be a session with parents discussing a revised format of reports in the light of proposed changes. Such involvement produces support and leads to much greater understanding of the assessment and reporting procedures followed by the school.

When formulating policies, involving pupils will also bring clear benefits. At the very least it will lead to greater understanding of what is expected of them. An example of such involvement could be if a school were to decide upon a new system of commendation which recognised particular achievement in agreed areas of school life. The school council or similar body of pupils could discuss the sorts of achievement which merited recognition and the areas of school life worthy of the scheme, such as service to the community, social skills displayed to others, or personal skills.

The purpose of assessment

Any statement regarding assessment must surely begin with statements of purpose, detailing the policy itself to ensure continuity of practice across the whole school and the purpose of assessment itself. While assessment will take many forms, each having different emphases, there are some important purposes which form consistent threads through all assessments:

For the pupil

- to provide learning goals

- to raise the level of motivation

For the teacher

– to obtain feedback for evaluation purposes

– to determine pupil's strengths and weaknesses

– as a means of indicating the achievement of learning objectives

For the parents

– to be informed of their children's progress and achievements.

Alternatively, a school may wish to define the purposes of assessment in terms of its formative, diagnostic, summative and evaluative functions.

Good practice

Having defined purpose, the following guiding principles of good practice can be agreed upon:

1. It is derived from clear curriculum intentions and learning objectives.

2. There is identification of the various activities through which learning objectives can be approached.

3. There is identification of the various forms of evidence produced.

4. There is a sensible recording system designed to inform pupils and parents of progress.

5. Pupils are fully aware of what is expected of them and they are involved in such activities as target setting/recording self-assessment.

6. It encourages pupils to aim for higher standards.

7. It encourages parents to take an active interest in the assessment of their children's progress.

Two very useful documents which highlight assessment success and failures are the DFE publications *Assessment, Recording and Reporting* – a report by HMI on the first year of the curricular requirements of ERA 1989–90, and *Education Observed, The Implementation of the Curricular Requirements of ERA, An Overview* by HM Inspectorate on the second year 1990–91. Though set in the context of an ill-conceived assessment model, they clearly identify those features of assessment which will be displayed in a successful school. Once such principles are established, assessment becomes an integral part of curriculum planning and development.

Marking

At the core of any assessment of pupils' work is the manner in which teachers mark. Again, there should be consensus as to the purpose of marking, and its motivating powers should be stressed. To both pupils and parents, marking is one of the clearest indications of the school's attitude towards its pupils. Marking conveys an image of the school not to be underestimated.

While it is impossible to mark every piece of a pupil's work to the same detail, there needs to be a clear, agreed policy which will among other things suggest criteria for marking particular pieces of work. Such criteria may be, for example, *effort*, with agreed statements of five or so levels of effort to be indicated on the work in an agreed manner. Likewise *attainment* will almost certainly be marked, but the referencing of attainment grades/marks needs to be consistent. Most schools now appear to criteria mark which leads to a more constructive verbal/written dialogue with pupils, judging their work against the learning objectives rather than the work of their peers. Again, agreement on the range of grades/marks and how they will be indicated on pupil's work is essential.

In any marking policy, clear emphasis should be put on the importance of constructive comments rather than simple ticks and overall scores. Further, such assessment should be discussed with pupils as soon as reasonably possible after completion.

A most useful guide for all teachers when marking is that of the basic 200 high-frequency words which should always be spelt correctly. Simple agreed statements such as having capital letters for proper nouns will help to create consistency across all departments.

Recording

From marking follows the recording process. With the massive paraphernalia of the SOA assessment model there was a danger of recording dictating the style of assessing. The mark book is still as central to the recording system as the pupil's exercise book/file is to the evidence which supports any assessment decision. That is not to say that all evidence is concrete – indeed, much is observed, reflected and discussed.

IT systems will have an essential role in, at the very least, the accumulation of records of assessment through the key stages. Such systems will enable reconciling the potential problem of the annual mark book with the continuous key stage assessment and thereby enabling genuine progression to take place. Schools will have to develop systems to meet their identified needs but would be wise to link such recording to well-established administrative systems such as SIMS which have the necessary databases of academic pupil information. This should not be inefficiently re-created in various departments; there must be one database only.

Evidence

There will have to be agreement concerning the nature of evidence to be retained. Indeed the question of evidence retention threatened to swamp recent assessment proposals. Clearly common sense will prevail, but schools will need to be able to justify decisions concerning pupil attainment using the evidence accumulated.

Decisions concerning achievements necessitate agreement of 'standards'. This issue is now all the more significant in light of the Dearing Interim Report which places teacher assessment alongside test outcomes in terms of status. Schools will have to devise their own policies for ensuring consistency across teaching groups and for ensuring that they meet the needs of whatever audit process is set into place. This is most likely to be based on either LEA's acting as audit agents working closely with individual or clusters of schools or on the GCSE style operation with groups or consortia of schools.

Naturally the assessment of pupils' work is central to any Record of Achievement (ROA). However, the difficult issue of linking the 'academic' assessment of pupils' work with the wider ROA process is still an area of debate. Having an ROA system alongside an academic assessment system is clearly wasteful of precious time. Through the data handling capacity of IT, the future may well lie in greater use of systems such as SIMS with pupil data being speedily merged from a variety of sources to a common output format and an overall picture of a pupil's total achievements being readily available.

Without a whole-school approach to assessment, which shares a common policy based on agreed principles, good practice will be lost and curriculum delivery will be inadequate.

References

Croner Head Teacher's Briefing, No 19 Nov 1992.

Interim Report. The National Curriculum and its Assessment, SEAC/ NCC, 1993.

The Handbook for Inspections of Schools, 1992.

The Implementation of the Curricular Requirements of the Education Reform Act *Assessment, Recording and Reporting*. A Report by HM Inspectorate on the first year, 1989–90, HMSO 1991.

Education Observed. The Implementation of the Curricular Requirements of ERA. An Overview by HM Inspectorate on the second year, 1990–91, HMSO 1992.

Managing School Visits

Chris Lowe

For many teachers the first contact with school management tasks beyond the classroom comes with their participation in the organisation of a school visit. It is surprising, therefore, how little attention has been paid to this issue in initial teacher training and in-service training. Indeed it took the deaths of pupils in the Lands End tragedy to galvanise many local education authorities (LEAs) and schools into producing policies and guidelines. After the inquiry into another tragedy, the deaths of five English schoolboys in the Alps, it was abundantly clear to LEAs and schools that all aspects of safety had to be thought out in advance and be well understood by those taking part. The most recent 1993 tragedy in Lyme Bay, when young canoeists in a school adventure training group were drowned, serves to underline the need for continual vigilance by school authorities. Absolute guarantees of safety are not possible, but good reconnaissance and efficient planning are essential ingredients.

It is not only the party's physical safety that has to be considered. Financial security is also an issue – never more so than in the past two years when so many tour companies have gone out of business. Whenever a tour company fails it is the school which has to pick up the pieces.

Responsibilities

For these reasons, all those concerned with the management of schools should be clear about their own duties and how they fit into the pattern of responsibilities for outside activities.

The legal responsibilities are summarised in Table 5.4.1.

Local authorities, while they remain the employers, are responsible for the actions of their employees in the course of their employment, particularly for their health and safety and for the proper discharge of their duties to pupils. LEAs are also under a duty to determine their policy for the school curriculum (subject to the National Curriculum regulations). They must also publish a charging and remissions policy.

Governing bodies of independent and grant-maintained schools have the same responsibility for the general conduct of the school and may also modify the LEA's policy on the curriculum, which could include extracurricular activities. Governing bodies of maintained schools are also obliged to have charging and remission policies. The head is responsible for seeing that these policies are implemented. Heads' conditions of employment in maintained schools include responsibility for ensuring that activites are properly planned and supervised, and that pupils' safety is paramount.

Teachers have a common-law duty to take reasonable care of pupils, as a reasonable parent would (ie *in loco parentis*). Under their conditions of employment they are also responsible for maintaining good order and discipline among the pupils and safeguarding their health and safety whether on or off school premises whenever they are engaged in authorised school activities.

Table 5.4.1 *A summary of legal responsibilities*

School policies

As part of the discharge of their duties, governors and heads usually produce a general policy which includes the following:

- a statement about the kind of visits allowed and to whom they should be accessible;

- a requirement that all activities should have stated aims in line with the school's curriculum aims;

- consultation requirements, eg with heads, parents and pupils;

- planning and organisational procedures;

- emergency procedures;

- code of safety and conduct expected;

- special needs considerations;

- financial procedures;

- insurance requirements; and

- evaluation and follow-up work.

Accompanying this should be the statutory charging and remissions policy set out in DES (now the DFE) Circular 1/89 Charging for School Activities.

Organisation

The actual organisation of any school outing goes through three key stages. At the initial consideration and *consultation* stage the head or a member of the senior management team who has responsibility should satisfy him/herself that the educational aim is acceptable, that the target groups are clear, that the organisers are sufficient and competent, and that they are in possession of the school's policies and procedures. Any special matters to be highlighted should also be apparent at this point – such as arrangements for any handicapped pupils, use of non-teachers, any extra insurance, the need for a preliminary visit.

Planning

The *planning* stage is largely a matter for the organisers. Many schools now have a checklist to aid the process and, apart from built-in reporting points to the senior management team, there is usually no need for interference.

It is an old army saying that 'time spent on reconnaissance is never wasted', and the best way to guarantee a safe and enjoyable visit is through sound policies and thorough planning. All this is discussed in detail in *Hobsons School Travel Organiser's Handbook*, which is sent annually to each school, free of charge. Further copies can be obtained from Hobsons Publishing, Europa House, St Matthew Street, London SW1 2JT. The *Staffroom Guide to School Visits*, published by EMAP, is also sent free to schools.

Running the visit is, of course, the prime duty of the organiser. Heads only become involved in emergencies. But even the actions to be taken in emergencies ought to have been thought through and included in school policies, along with other advice on safety matters.

Negligence

One of the major concerns of all organisers of school activities is the question of negligence. Teachers rightly seek reassurance that they will not be liable if any accident occurs. Although it is not possible to lay down hard and fast rules to avoid being sued for negligence, the general principles are clear. They stem from the concept of 'the duty of care' that a teacher owes to children. The standard of care that the teacher must display is that of a prudent and careful parent, ie teachers are said to be *in loco parentis* (in place of a parent). Although parents do not normally have ten or more children to look after on an outing, the consideration of their welfare and safety must be that which the absent parent would consider reasonable. Clearly this is a difficult area and begs a lot of questions. However, it is rare for an accusation of negligence to be sustained against teachers, who are known to be very careful by nature and training. Heads can help to allay fears by putting into place good policies and good procedures backed up by sound advice and training. If an organiser follows tried and tested procedures then it would be very unlikely that a court would find him/her negligent. Courts recognise that 'accidents do happen' despite the best laid plans.

LEAs and governors or school proprietors, as employers, are ultimately responsible for any actions of their employees which are done in the course of their employment and which constitute negligence. The onus is, therefore, on them to see that employees are well-trained and the activities well-planned.

Evaluation

The final evaluation stage can often get lost once the euphoria of a visit has worn off. The senior management team should ensure that this does not happen. Not only is it important educationally for staff and pupils to reflect on the knowledge and experience gained, but a well-designed evaluation pro forma and debriefing procedure may well enable the running of future visits to be that little bit better. Such an evaluation form for staff and students should include headings such as:

- comments on the preplanning and preliminary information
- suitability of the venue
- comments on accommodation and food
- reception at venues (or by host families in the case of exchange visits)
- problems faced
- benefits gained

The comments should be scrutinised by the head or a senior manager with delegated responsibility, and knowledge gleaned should inform regular, though not necessarily frequent, monitoring of the whole system. Reports to the governing body will enable members to consider, commend or amend their own policy. Governing bodies may also include a reference to the running of school visits in prospectuses and annual reports to parents.

A well-oiled school visits procedure, known and appreciated by governors, staff and parents, can have a quite disproportionate effect on the respect for a school's ethos and its efficiency. Equally, the opposite is true.

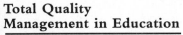

Part Six

Managing External Relations

Marketing for Schools

David Pardey

Why is marketing relevant to schools?

Is it a direct outcome of LMS?

Local Management of Schools (LMS) has created the educational marketplace, making each school autonomous, serving two inter-related markets. The first is the Education Authority which 'buys' places, mainly in cash but partly through the provision of some services 'in kind'. The second market is the 'decider/user' market – the parents and their children whose collective decisions and experiences determine whether or not the school is able to generate the funding it needs.

Grant-maintained status (GMS) takes this a stage further, replacing this funding customer with another, paying wholly in cash. The attraction to secondary schools of the GM option should not blind them to the demands this new customer places or will place on them.

But isn't marketing about aggressive competition?

The market for schools is finite; the growth of one must be at the expense of another. Incorporation of FE and VI form Colleges has created a far more competitive environment for schools with sixth forms, which might have led to a breakdown in co-operative arrangements. Marketing has been blamed for this since it is aggressive promotion and sales activity which is often used to influence decision-making.

The problem is that marketing is a very flexible word; it can just mean selling, promotion and aggressive competition, or it can mean making the market's requirements central to decision-making. If the market is looking for particular choices which are more easily available through co-operation than competition, then co-operation reflects a more market-led approach.

Putting the market at the centre of the school's decision-making means serving the needs of pupils, their parents and the community. This is associated with the 'social market', an attempt to merge the principles of the market economy with the goals of the public sector. The social market only has meaning if it involves serving a social purpose; marketing done properly doesn't subvert the school's mission, it furthers it.

Isn't marketing about making a profit?

The Chartered Institute of Marketing defines marketing as being about 'identifying, anticipating and satisfying customers' requirements at a profit' but this narrow idea is now overtaken by the development of an 'alternative' marketing for non-profit-making organisations. This needs a clear purpose in place of profit; for this reason, the starting point for any school in establishing its marketing strategy must be to define its 'mission' – in management guru Peter Drucker's words, 'what business are we in?'.

Do you know what kind of school you want to be?

What is your mission? Do you have a shared vision?

Do you really know what kind of school you want to be? A broad-based institution serving the needs of a wide-ranging market, or a highly specialised one, catering for pupils with learning difficulties or for those motivated to learn music, science or technology – a 'niche strategy'.

A niche market may be a smaller one; it is important for schools to recognise that there are other measures of success than size. A commitment to a minority market need might mean downsizing, so the mission of an institution helps to define the market and how success will be measured. It is essential that the governors, managers and staff know what the school is aiming to do and are behind those goals and values. This is the 'internal Marketing' task – identifying the aspriations of others within the school and matching these to what the school wants to do to.

Are your goals realistic, achievable?

Know your market geographically, demographically, socially, economically and ethnically. What do people want from the school, and how does that match up against what you want provide? The power that the new market gives people is not exercised equally by all its members, so seek out, listen to and respond to the requirements of all members of the community. Set targets for:

- market penetration – how many pupils from each market segment?;

- performance – what the school will offer them?; and

- outcomes – what they should achieve.

The opportunity to take up the city technology college (CTC) banner which is now available to GM schools opens up new market opportunities and threats. Are there sufficient parents and children in your local market who would be attracted by the science and technology emphasis of the CTC model? Can your institution satisfy the market with the provision you can offer?

Are you the kind of school you and the market want you to be?

Does reality match rhetoric?

Marks and Spencer illustrates the way in which long-term market success is achieved through commitment to commonly understood goals and minimal advertising. In a survey of consumer's impressions of major companies, 60 per cent people who thought Marks and Spencer had a distinctive voice said this was because of the firm's high-quality products. Their success is built on doing what they say they are going to do and allowing their reputation to promote them. Every satisfied customer reinforces that reputation until the next purchase, but one dissatisfied customer can be lost forever and with that one customer may go many others.

Schools rely primarily on their reputations and those reputations are being reinforced or destroyed every day. The ability of the school to live up to the image it wishes to project is essential no amount of glossy publicity can counteract one bad experience by a parent or pupil (or by a friend, colleague, friend of a colleague, etc).

What benefits does the market look for?

A customer seeks benefits, not products; it is not how a product is produced that matters but the benefit it provides. You must find out from your market what benefits they seek, and then provide and promote them. Don't say 'The school operates a pastoral care system, each pupil having a personal tutor with responsibility for negotiating an individual learning contract, entered in their Record of Achievement'.

Instead, say 'One teacher has responsibility for your child's performance and will be in constant touch with her/him. You (the parent) can contact that teacher at these times to discuss your child's progress.' Those are the benefits that derive from the system and that will influence the 'purchase' decision.

Listen to the market. Don't use open days/evenings to harangue parents; let them ask you questions. The more opportunities parents and their children have to experience what the school is about, the more the school is able to find out their demands. Market research is about knowing your market by using all available sources of data. It doesn't just mean questionnaires and surveys; it means talking to people and listening to what they have to say.

Can you communicate effectively?

How do you promote the school?

Promotion can be expensive, particularly when it is done badly or when the image being promoted is not consistent with what the school is actually like. Table 6.1.1 gives some simple rules which should be followed.

- Decide who the promotion is aimed at and what it is designed to achieve (what are you expecting people *to do* as a result?)

- Keep it simple, use images (pictures and graphics) rather than words as far as possible.

- Colour is expensive but adds impact when used well. For economy, a better quality paper or the limited use of a second colour (spot colour) can add a lot for little extra cost.

- Stress the benefits – not the process – using simple, short sentences addressed to the reader (second person, active voice).

Table 6.1.1 *Simple rules for promotion*

What image do you project?

Changing perceptions is difficult and expensive. You must start with what you have already got and build on that. Avis car rentals built up an international business on not being number one in their industry 'We try harder' is their slogan. You need to stand back from your school and look at it, warts and all; listen to what people say about it; and, knowing what you want to achieve, set out to build on that. If the school is new, stress modernity and the future; if it's old, you can stress tradition and solidity.

The image of the school is created by first impressions; ask a friend to pose as a new parent and tell you what he/she experienced to get an objective picture. Above all, be aware that changing perceptions of the school is a long haul and is only possible if there is substance along with desired image.

Tim King, managing director of Siegel and Gale, a corporate identity consultancy, stresses the two simple rules in Table 6.1.2 for getting through the clutter of communications and speaking to people with a clear voice.

Jill Forster of The Body Shop says: 'The Body Shop is a successful communicator because we will never compromise our values . . . We have never diluted our image, we know our strengths and we are not frightened to shout our beliefs from the rooftops.'

- If you have any distinctive and relevant values make them the core of your communications.
- Understand how people's impressions are formed. You can spend far less money to greater effect if you learn how and where to spend it.

Table 6.1.2 *Simple rules for a clear voice*

How do you ensure a good relationship with the media?

Your local media will be constantly on the look-out for any story that has human interest, whether it be humorous, calamitous or exceptional. Regular, positive coverage in a local paper or on local radio comes by making personal contact and finding out what the medium is looking for. With exam results, a newspaper will want a story to make sense of the dry statistics, so if you have a catchment area which makes exam success problematic, find an individual success story and build that into a newsworthy story.

How should you manage marketing?

Who does what?

The headteacher and governors have shared responsibility for setting the strategic direction of the school while functional activities can easily be delegated once targets have been agreed. Who does what is essentially a question of who is most able to undertake the various tasks required – not the person who is least employed and most easily spared!

A marketing plan is a simple way of setting down your goals and the strategies for achieving them. The school development plan is the right place to incorporate one, including market analysis, market objectives and the marketing strategy. In a larger school particularly, with a more substantial budget and divided responsibilities for the various functional areas, there is a real need for a marketing plan to ensure that there is a co-ordinated and focused strategy.

How much should you spend?

As little as possible but as much as is necessary! Once you have decided what you want to achieve and how you intend to achieve it, then you should look at how much that will cost. If the cost is too high you must decide whether there is a cheaper way of achieving your goals and, if not, which goals will be sacrificed. There is no formula other than clear objectives, accurate costing and informed judgement.

Further reading

Managing an organisation in a market-led way:
Drucker, P (1991), *Management: Tasks, Responsibilities, Practices*, Butterworth Heinemann.
Making an organisation enthusiastically responsive to the market:
Kanter, R M (1985), *The Change Masters: Corporate Entrepreneurs at Work*, Unwin.
The principles of marketing and their application to schools:
Pardey, D (1991), *Marketing for Schools*, Kogan Page.

6.2

Reporting to Parents and Parental Links

John Dunford

Legal obligations

As with so many areas of education, reporting to parents has become a legal obligation. A school's desire to report to parents on children's progress through its own methods has become a burdensome duty, laid down by legislation in immense detail. The relevant documents are:

- Education (Individual Pupils' Achievements) (Information) Regulations 1992

- DFE Circular 14/92, superseded by Circular 7/93

The detailed obligations placed on schools by these documents leave little room for flexibility, but these requirements are only part of the practice of good reporting to parents. And reporting is only one aspect of the wider issue of links between home and school.

The school development plan

The triangle of co-operation between the school, the parent and the pupil forms such an important part of a school's success that it must be at the core of the aims of the institution. All schools are sufficiently keen to improve their relations with parents that the issue is almost certain to form part of every school development plan.

A home–school partnership contract

Some schools have formalised the obligations of both parents and teachers into a home–school partnership contract, which will have been adopted by the governing body and is usually signed by the head and the parent. In the contract, the school agrees to such obligations as:

- to promote the best possible learning atmosphere for everyone;

- to record attendance and inform parents of any irregularities; and

- to invite parents to discuss matters of concern.

The parent agrees to a similar range of obligations:

- to keep their child in regular and punctual attendance;

- to support the code of conduct of the school; and

- to keep in contact with the school regarding the child's progress.

Schools give much thought to the induction of pupils. How many schools have a policy on the induction of *parents*? Considerable thought is given to the school prospectus as a marketing tool, but it is also important as part of the induction process.

- Is the prospectus written in accessible language, avoiding jargon?

- Does it convey the intended messages about partnership with parents?

- Does it mention all the links between home and school?

- What does it say about the extent of parental involvement in the school?

Parent consultation meetings

Parent consultation meetings usually occur at least once a year. Considerable thought is given to the dates and timing of these events, and other ways of increasing the attendance of parents. One area which is often ignored is the wording of the letters of invitation which, like the prospectus, must be welcoming, clear and free from educational jargon.

The telephone

The telephone is a vital link between home and school, yet it can be a cruelly impersonal instrument. The way in which a school answers its telephone calls and guides the callers to the right person says much about the institution. If the right person is not available, the school must ensure that someone with authority can always be contacted – some crises cannot wait until the next break-time.

School-to-home communication

When pupils begin to have problems at school and parents need to be notified, the telephone is usually the best mode of contact. A policy on home visits by teachers is necessary. This may be only for more serious cases or for families where it is impossible for the parents to visit the school. Some schools benefit greatly from a regular programme of home visits, but this is expensive and may not be possible in many catchment areas. Programmes can be held at surgeries in areas from which it is difficult for parents to come in to the school.

The newsletter remains the most common form of regular communication from school to parent. There is no magic formula to ensure that these pieces of paper arrive at their destinations and do not languish at the bottom of the school bag. Whether weekly, monthly or termly, a regular date of issue is helpful. The content of the newsletter includes dates of holidays, school events, parent consultation evenings, PTA evenings and important deadlines, well in advance. It includes achievements by individuals and groups in the school. It should have an informative educational content too, explaining curriculum and organisational changes in a way that parents will understand. Many schools are now using homework diaries and other types of contact book. These can be an excellent way of maintaining regular contact between home and school with a focus on work set and standards achieved.

The governing body

The parent representatives on the governing body are key people in the home-school partnership. If they are prepared to spend the necessary time on their governorship, they are an excellent conduit of parental opinion to the school and of school issues to the parents.

They must be kept well informed and should be given the opportunity, perhaps through the newsletter, to communicate with parents.

The governors' official organ of communication and accountability is the annual report to parents, in which they recount the results of their stewardship. Many of these reports are incredibly boring and seem to be designed expressly to prevent parents from taking an interest in the school. Nor do they always encourage parents to attend the governors' annual meeting itself. The annual report and annual meeting, which are both statutory requirements, are not among the government's great legislative successes of the 1980s, but they can be made into a useful part of the school's involvement of parents. They can also be used as a good opportunity to prepare parents for a forthcoming inspection.

Parents as helpers

School PTAs have more than a fund-raising purpose. If supported by the head and senior management, the PTA can provide good opportunities to bring parents into school. Most of these occasions are social or educational meetings and the opportunity for parents and teachers to work together with a common purpose is very valuable. The PTA also provides schools with a group of willing adults whose assistance can be used in other ways. Indeed, some schools have an active policy of using adults other than teachers (AOTs) in the classroom situation. Where this involves the planning of the lesson as an integral part of the course – and not as a one-off presentation – it is especially effective. A survey of parents can be used to establish a list of AOTs who have relevant skills and knowledge.

Records of achievement and reports to parents

Questionnaires and surveys to parents can be used to check on all aspects of home–school relations. It is useful, for example, to know how helpful and comprehensible the parents find the school's records of achievement and written reports on their children. This helps to reveal whether the school is communicating the information which it thinks it is giving. If the school uses both records of achievement and written reports, the links between them must be clear and gradings must be consistent.

One of the advantages of records of achievement is that they contain positive comments; any negative remarks are conveyed as targets for future achievement. This is much less discouraging than the put-downs which used to be so prevalent in school reports.

One word which has to be treated with great care is 'satisfactory'. Both school and parent must be clear whether it represents a positive or a negative comment; if this is not clear, the word is better avoided altogether.

In secondary school reports, consistency between subjects and different teachers is also important. Grade B from one teacher in PE must convey the same level of achievement as grade B from another teacher in History. The meaning of the grades, for both attainment and effort, must be explained clearly at the start of the report and the grading system should be related to the national curriculum grading pattern.

While the government has concentrated on the mechanistic reporting of attainment, teachers have continued to communicate information to parents in a more discursive way. This is an important part of the growing range of communications between school and home. The objective must remain not only the involvement of parents in the education process, but above all the sensitive encouragement of the standard of achievement of the individual child.

Enterprise in Education – A Programme for the 90s

Laurence French

Schools have long been in the business of raising money for themselves, but it is only in recent years that schools have been 'in business' in the way they are managed and financed.

As the recession has bitten deeper and the economy declined, the amount of money in the system has been reduced and funds far more difficult to come by. However, money is available if you know where to look for it. This article is intended to point out the ways in which schools can maximise their marketing potential so that funds can be gained and sponsorship increased.

What is sponsorship?

It can be any or all of the following:

- financial income: (a) gifts and donations, (b) covenants, (c) regular payments into school's bank account;

- time: companies paying for their employees' time to come into school for a variety of reasons;

- facilities: the availability of a company's facilities for school use, and vice versa;

- expertise: the use of business/industrial experts by a school;

- equipment: the donation of equipment by a company for school use;

- events: the support (financial or otherwise) of a school event by a company;

- secondments: staff being seconded to business for training or work experience.

We can see that sponsorship is far more wide-ranging than simply asking for money to contribute to school funds. While it can be a very important part of your school's income generation programme, it is by no means the only way. If you are going to enter the enterprise culture, you need to give consideration to a much more comprehensive programme – one which will elicit more constant flow of funds over a long period. We are not talking here of short-termism.

Going grant-maintained

Without doubt, one of the major ways in which a school can increase its income and use its budget in a more cost effective manner is for it to go GM. The whole area of funding for GM schools is complicated and full discussion of it here is not possible. However, outlined below are some of the main benefits that a school can expect.

'Enterprise in Education', an organisation which conducts seminars around the country on fundraising, has done a case study of the effects of GM status on a school of 1,106 students. The following is a summary of the main additional grants that a GM school can expect on an annual basis:

(a) In-service training, governor training, curriculum development – this grant is worth £42.50 per pupil.

(b) Minor Capital Allocations – This is worth £10,000 per school and £20 per pupil.

(c) A rate saving of around £58,441, as GM schools are liable for only 20 per cent of their rates bill due to charitable status.

(d) Section 11, Technical and Vocational Education Initiative (TVEI) and similar initiatives – grants are paid directly to the school rather than through the Council. The school can therefore bid directly for these funds.

Additional grants are also available to GM schools. A transitional grant (a one-off) is worth £30,000 plus £30 per pupil. The other main one is the restructuring grant for retirements or redundancy payments as well as staff training for the new status. Although no specific figure is available, 'Enterprise in Education' estimates it to be between £30,000 and £40,000. Taking into account the likely increase in pupil numbers that a GM school can expect, the financial gain can be approximately £500,000 to £700,000.

Maximising the potential of your school

Other methods of fund-raising and income generation are more likely to be attractive to the non-GM schools. The key to the success of such ventures is your ability to maximise the potential of the school and its facilities.

Try walking around the school to see what facilities are being under-used or neglected and which could be enhanced by fund-raising ventures. Many secondary schools, for example, have rather bare walls in their corridors. These spaces can be turned into cash. Local companies or the careers service might be interested in renting space in order to promote their product or service, the history of their company, opportunities for young people in that area of work and so on. A professionally produced display (done for you by the company), with properly mounted posters can turn a drab wall into something attractive, as well as producing some much-needed income. The spin-offs can be extensive too if you realise that your school has a 'commodity' that business needs – its future workforce. It could also open a number of possibilities for links with the company: teacher/industry exchanges; work experience for the pupils; work shadowing for staff. Application to your local Training and Enterprise Council (TEC) (or Local Enterprise Company (LEC) in Scotland) might elicit a grant which will match any monetary sponsorship by industry and commerce. This will, of course, depend on the financial position of the local TEC.

Other areas of the school might well have money-making potential too. With the excess capacity in many schools, some areas might be lying unused. With an investment of time and money they could be turned into a resource that can be used by the community, local firms or voluntary organisations. These spaces could be used for a variety of purposes:

• training

• meetings

• community ventures

• shared facilities for IT

- storage

- rehearsal rooms for local drama/music societies.

One major and significantly under-used asset that all schools possess is its Hall. Consider the potential within this area: a stage, lighting, seating for between 200 and 600 people, partitions, sound equipment and so on. Now consider what use is made of it during normal working hours – probably very little. All of these assets are worth money if they are marketed properly. At my school, Campion School, we printed a Site and Facilities Guide which is sent out to potential customers interested in hiring our premises.

The following is a list of some of the major uses to which you can put your Hall:

- venue for drama productions – touring companies, amateur dramatic societies and the like;

- making the most of productions that you put on yourself – good quality productions, attractive programmes, creative refreshments (in keeping with the period of the play, for example), publicity, media interest, parental involvement, student participation at all levels;

- weddings and reception facilities;

- discos – watch the security aspects though;

- rehearsal facilities for local drama, music groups;

- training facility for small- medium-sized companies;

- community meeting place – ideal for talks, lectures, performance;

- indoor sports – aerobics, badminton etc;

- cinema club for the school or local community;

- exhibitions and product launches – excellent for school/industry links. Needs to be prepared thoroughly and marketed extensively. Big money earner;

- bingo, karaoke, tea dances, quiz night.

Once the process starts you will be able to add to the list depending on your own circumstances and locality.

Such heavy use of the school premises does take its toll and one of the first things to be considered is the cleaning and caretaking aspect, as well as security and insurance implications.

If all this can be gained from the Hall, think what can be gained from the use of other rooms and areas such as the sports hall, refectory, specialist areas (technology, art, home economics), swimming pool, football/rugby pitches, all-weather sports areas and so on. The simple truth is that your school is a money-making concern if you know how to market it effectively.

Selling the skills

Alongside the facilities in your school, you have people who have skills which are marketable and income-generating. A skills audit of the staff is a useful way of finding out what they can offer. These could range from IT skills, word-processing, printing facilities, photocopying, library facilities, PR and marketing, training, cookery and catering, designing and scene painting for theatre productions. In these days of schools as business enterprises, it might become a profitable venture to set up in-school consultancies and sell the skills to other schools or companies at a much more competitive rate than could be bought from other consultants or agencies. This sort of thing could range from training staff to run their own training programmes (training the trainers), appraisal training, pre-inspection sessions, PR and marketing strategies and so on. Try employing a professional PR consultant and compare the cost! Under this system you use the GEST money of other schools as a major income generating area for your school. GM schools are always better off in this respect getting £42.50 per pupil and not having to worry about the LEA either.

Grant grabbing

There's usually a source of money somewhere if you know where to look for it. GM schools are better placed when it comes to getting grants directly rather than having to go through the LEA first. Some of these were discussed earlier in this article. However, grants are available whatever type of school you are. If you are in the business of grant grabbing you will need to differentiate between being a recipient of the grant or a producer of services for other school's grants as suggested above. The following information is courtesy of 'Enterprise in Education':

1. GEST funding is a major source of grants for schools both as consumers and providers of services. Schools should be aware of the various headings under which GEST funding is given. This

information can be gained from DFE circular 13 August 1992 (tel: 071 925 6080). This will detail headings and criteria.

2. DTI Enterprise in Education Scheme – providing money for learning systems and equipment (tel: 0800 800 432). Money has been given for training access for the industrial and commercial sector.

3. Training and Enterprise Grants (TEGs) – will often match financial sponsorship by industry and commerce. There are a number of other grants available from TECs, particularly concerning training and links with business and commerce.

4. Further Education Funding Council and Adult Education grants – can be gained by developing vocational training programmes with FE sector and non-vocational adult education courses held at schools.

5. European Social Fund – for training of adults and young people. GM schools can bid directly, but LMS schools could link with FE or HE institutions.

6. LINGUA – grants available to assist exchanges of foreign language students and teachers (tel: 071 224 1477).

7. Central Bureau of the DFE – grants available for travel scholarships and bursaries (tel: 071 486 5101).

8. Sports Council Grants – for the development of sporting facilities, especially those for community use.

Legal considerations regarding sponsorship

There are a number of legal points that should be borne in mind when seeking sponsorship:

- There must be a declaration by any member of the school having financial interests in the sponsoring company. Failure to do so can lead to very unfortunate publicity or legal action.

- Any financial benefits derived from sponsorship must be itemised in the school accounts for the auditors.

- You need to be aware of copyright legislation in any literature that is being reproduced about your school or sponsoring company.

- If you enter into a sponsorship deal, a legal contract protects both parties. A solicitor will advise you on this.

- Be sure to take steps to protect your reputation should things go wrong.

- Insurance – if the school is sponsoring an event, are non-teachers protected under your insurance policy or by their own company's?

- Insurance for equipment – who is covered for what and for how much?

- If a member of staff is seconded to a company, check that they are covered under the company's employee insurance scheme.

And finally . . . some words from Tom Peters:

> If you are not reconfiguring your organisation to become fast-changing, high value-adding creator of niche markets, you are simply out of step . . .'
> (*Thriving On Chaos*)

The same applies to schools.

Useful publications and organisations

Fitzherbert, L and Eastwood, M (ed) *A Guide to Major Trusts*
Norton, M (ed) *A Guide to Company Giving*
(Both books available from local libraries or from: The Directory of Social Change, Radius Works, Back Lane, London NW3 1HL.)

Enterprise in Education
40 Parc-y-Felin, Creigiau, Cardiff CF4 8BP. Tel: 0222 890770.

International Links

Peter Downes

Few educationists would deny the rapidly growing importance of the international dimension in our schools today. Most of those we are educating today will live in an international world in a way that few of their parents or grandparents will have experienced. Greater possibilities of foreign travel, increased trading opportunities and rapidly developing communication systems are all combining to break down the traditional insularity of the British. Whereas, in the past, international links were restricted to the colonial elite and a small fraction of the trading and academic community, in the future there is a much greater chance that young people will work abroad, or alongside 'foreigners' in this country, will carry out part of their training or education abroad, will take holidays abroad more readily and will inter-marry with people of different nations.

The responsibility for preparing pupils and students for this new world lies predominantly with the school. The difficulty we face is knowing how to move on from a general feeling of goodwill towards the international dimension into doing something practical to make it come alive. This chapter will suggest activities both for pupils and for teachers (including heads and deputies) for, without a commitment on the part of the professional leaders, very little of practical value will be achieved.

Raising awareness within the school

Some of the following practical ideas are obviously 'superficial' while others will take more time and demand greater input:

- If your school has a flag-pole, buy some foreign flags and fly them on the appropriate national day (most diaries have a list of these) or when you have a foreign visitor.

- Use one of the notice-board areas in your school for a frequently changing display of foreign countries, with large-scale maps and photographs. Art, design and geography departments could collaborate on this.

- Suggest that each form or tutor-group in the school 'adopts' a foreign country, does some research about it and displays it on part of the classroom notice-board. It is possible for schools to link with each other by fax through, for example, the European Secondary Heads Association (ESHA) network (see later) so that regular information can be exhanged with countries where a conventional exchange or correspondence is not possible.

- For older pupils interested in debating, set up a mini-United Nations Organisation Security Council or a European Parliament and get them to debate a current issue by playing the part and trying to defend the views of different countries.

- If you have a sympathetic catering manager, have an occasional special menu day where the food will be linked to a specified country.

- It may be possible to arrange a social event round the theme of international awareness, perhaps focused on Europe at first, with quizzes and party-games with an international dimension.

- Assemblies can be used to promote an international perspective, with readings from the writings of great men and women from different countries, with slides or music if available. Many of the new anthologies of assemblies contain good material along these lines and can be made to fall within the national curriculum requirements for most of the time.

Links for pupils

Exchange visits. These remain an ideal way of increasing international awareness, although there are obvious practical and financial difficulties in carrying out exchanges with remote countries. It is most important that pupils going on foreign exchanges should be thoroughly prepared and de-briefed afterwards. Such are the logistical tasks faced by teacher organisers that they tend to neglect the content of the visit, assuming that participants will benefit

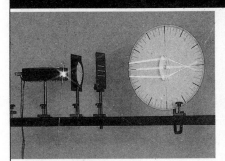

merely by travelling abroad. Many organisations exist to put schools in contact with each other (see the list of useful addresses at the end of this chapter).

Correspondence. A generation ago this was a question of the laborious process of collecting in letters and waiting a long time for replies. Today there are many options, for example, correspondence by fax, video and e-mail enables individuals or classes to be in touch with each other in a much more interesting and varied way.

Hosting. Depending on which part of the country you live in, there are sometimes opportunities for hosting young people from abroad who have come over to learn English. This can be done on a voluntary or on a paying basis.

Work experience. Sixth Formers may be able to plan for their work experience to take place abroad and, although it has not been possible in the past to attract LINGUA funding to support this, it is hoped that there will be a greater chance of financial support for post-16 students not directly involved in vocational studies.

Cross-curricular projects. It is most important to try to break the subconscious exclusive connection between the international dimension and the modern languages department. A number of fascinating cross-curricular projects involving geography, history, science and art departments have been carried out and will shortly be reported on in detail in a publication from the Council of Europe.

Study visits. These too can be based round an area of the curriculum not directly linguistic. A trip to see the battlefields of the First World War in Northern France, or to Normandy to see the Second World War beaches and the Bayeux Tapestry can be both historically and linguistically enriching. A well-organised visit to Paris can cover history, art, science, architecture and media studies with or without the linguistic component. Study visits further afield, including the USA and Russia, are orgnised with great success by a number of schools.

Links for teachers

The likelihood of a school commitment to the international diemnsion is much enhanced if teachers, including the head and the deputy, can be involved.

Exchange for teachers. These are arranged by the Central Bureau for Exchanges and Visits and have the double advantage of giving a

British teacher a chance to broaden his or her horizons and at the same time brings a foreign presence into the school in the form of the exchanging teacher. It is most important, however, that the induction of the incoming teacher is given high priority by the Senior Management Team as the expectations of British schools vary considerably from those in other countries and it is best to clarify these early on so as to avoid embarrassment at a later stage.

Study visits. A number of organisations offer teachers, heads and deputies the chance to spend a week or fortnight 'shadowing' in an overseas school. A great deal can be learnt in a short time and the cross-fertilisation of ideas is beneficial to all. Cambridgeshire LEA arranged for all its secondary heads to spend a weekend in Germany, sharing a two-day conference with German heads, followed by two days work shadowing. The following year the German heads returned to Cambridgeshire on a similar basis. This project was felt to be most helpful; ironically, it is the kind of enterprise which it will become increasingly difficult to fund as LEAs lose schools to the grant-maintained sector and are required to delegate more and more of their INSET funding to schools.

Conferences for heads. The International Confederation of Principals and the European Secondary Heads Association (to which both SHA and NAHT are affiliated) both organise major gatherings from time to time. While these admittedly have a direct effect on only that small minority of heads and deputies able to take part, their influence can be spread more widely as good ideas are disseminated through Heads' Associations in the various participating countries. As with all conferences, it is the contacts made informally that often have as much effect as the formal set-piece sessions. Those interested in forthcoming conferences should contact the addresses given later.

The linguistic factor

Traditional British linguistic incompetence has often been cited as an inhibiting factor in developing international links. As English becomes ever more firmly entrenched as the lingua franca, there is no need to allow linguistic barriers to stand in the way of valuable developments. At the same time, it is essential that linguistic skills and awareness are promoted in pupils and staff. The national curriculum requires continued study of a language to the age of 16 and it is not impossible that this requirement will be extended to 18 if some form of baccalaureate examination is introduced in this country. Just as important as a good working knowledge of at least one language is the understanding of how to learn a language quickly. Many of our pupils will need to learn languages for special purposes later in their lives; learning how to learn is therefore vital.

Conclusion

In this chapter it has only been possible to give a brief glimpse of the international opportunities available. As internal circumstances become more difficult in our own country, it will be tempting to concentrate on day-to-day survival and to leave the rest of the world to look after itself. To do so will be to sell our pupils short.

Further reading

Making the Most of Your Partner School Abroad Central Bureau for Educational Visits and Exchanges.

Policy Models: A Guide to Developing and Implementing European Dimension Policies in LEAs, Schools and Colleges Department for Education.

Hart, M *The European Dimension in General Primary and Seondary Education* Centre for International Education, c/o CEVNO, Nassau-plein 8, 1815 GM Alkmaar, The Netherlands (Tel: 010 31 72 11 85 02).

McLean, M (1990) *Britain and a Single Market Europe: Prospects for a Common School Curriculum* Kogan Page.

Part Seven

Managing Property, Premises and Resources

Facilities Management – A Coordinated Approach to Ancillary Services

David Cook

Facilities management, when applied to a school or college, means separating out those services which are ancillary to the core task of teaching. Such services should be managed cohesively in order to give added value to the teaching process, rather than become an intrusion.

A simple analysis (see Table 7.1.1) shows that there are many activities necessary for the delivery of education which are not directly part of the interaction between teacher and pupil (A). These can be further divided between those which are core management tasks (B) and those which are not (C).

In spite of this simple analysis it is evident that many head-teachers still spend a disproportionate amount of their time on such ancillary services. Facilities management offers the opportunity for heads to divest themselves of detailed involvement with these matters.

In Lincolnshire we have been examining facilities management as a practical option for schools. The original idea would have seen heads buying in from a single source the management and delivery of grounds maintenance, cleaning, catering, caretaking, security, etc. Heads would have a single budget line to manage against a single clear specification of quantity and quality. The contractor would be able to optimise overheads, use staff flexibly between services and reduce costs, hopefully to be reflected in an overall reduced cost for the client.

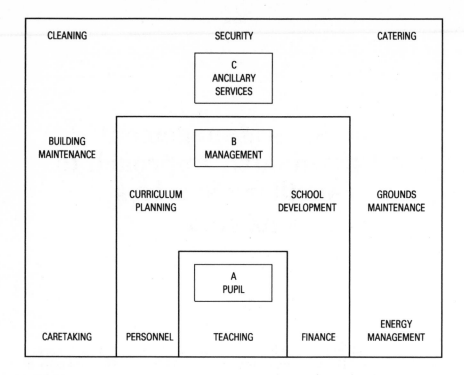

Table 7.1.1 *Some of the activities necessary for the delivery of education*

Unfortunately we have found little evidence of contractors with the experience or organisation to deliver services in this manner. Most are linked to a particular discipline, perhaps cleaning or catering, and so would have to sub-contract the remaining areas. We have modified our original concept for another reason as well. It would have placed a single contractor in an overly powerful position, akin to a monopoly, with all the potential dangers of such a situation. It is for this reason, more than any other, that few private sector organisations have chosen this method of procurement.

There is an alternative, which seems increasingly to make sense for the education market. That is to buy in the expert services of an independent third party in order to review the delivery of ancillary services. There are so many complications assocatied with compulsory competitive tendering, contracts generally, that this route must merit more consideration. The team commissioned for this purpose must have knowledge of school needs and of the individual ancillary services.

Each of these activities has its own technical requirements. Those requirements, and the associated technology, are constantly changing. Such developments can offer benefits to schools, but only if they have clearly established themselves as clients, and have not become immersed in the daily practicalities of getting the job done. Not seeing the wood for the trees is a common management failing.

There is a well-established trend for public services towards becoming 'enablers'. This means concentrating attention on the strategic responsibilities of the organisation, assessing the need for services, and then commissioning them. Managers in general are increasingly focusing on the planning of core activities, with areas peripheral to these being transferred to third parties. The enabling model may be equally applicable to the management of a school or college. There are several advantages to this approach:

1. Heads and senior school management can devote more of their valuable education expertise and management time to essential leadership and management tasks.

2. School staff do not usually have the expertise necessary to deal effectively with these services at a detailed level.

3. There are links and cross benefits between these services; improvements in value for money are possible by looking at them together, rather than in separate pigeon holes. Taking this approach is also more likely to lead to a packaging of services which is economical and reflects the real needs of the school. Packaging can involve a combination of arrangements from employing staff directly (the in-house option) to external contracting, and can break down the dividing lines between different activities.

4. Any change in one of these services can have knock-on effects for the others; security and cleaning, catering and energy management, etc. For example, how many heads will have considered the possibility of cleaning taking place for longer periods through the night at a large school, and the various benefits which this can bring, not only in terms of reduced cleaning costs but also for security?

5. Whilst involving themselves in the day-to-day management and administration of these services, school managers are less likely to step back and take an objective view of the services they are getting for their money.

It is likely that few schools will have seriously analysed their needs for services such as cleaning, maintenance, caretaking, etc. Some of these will have been subjected to competitive tendering, and schools then tend to stick with the original specification. That specification,

which is the main determinant of the price to be paid, may well have been prepared by a local authority in order to cover many different schools and premises. In that case it will not reflect the up-to-date and individual needs of any one school.

Whether a school is operating under GMS or LMS there is a tendency to carry on with existing service arrangements, inherited from an earlier regime, perhaps including the same contractor. Yet, in our experience, there are significant benefits to be gained, both in quality and price, from reviewing those arrangements. Even where contractual obligations have to be honoured there is always scope for such a review. Often existing contractors will be only too happy to cooperate in such an exercise. It is in their long term interests to adapt their services to the client's needs. Most professional contractors would prefer to work with an informed and discerning client. If an existing contractor will not make reasonable adjustments, then it is time to think about other options. Buying out the current contractor may be expensive, but such costs need to be measured against potential cost and quality benefits from a new deal, which better reflects the school's circumstances.

So it is not impossible to break out of present arrangements and move away from the *ad hoc* approach to ancillary services. When looked at together these services account for a sizeable proportion of any school's budget and they are capable of being refined and changed relatively easily compared, for example, to staffing costs.

In order to take this holistic approach to ancillary services and put in place an effective and economical new deal, the client needs time to tackle the exercise, expertise to understand the operational realities of the services, and skills for negotiating and evaluating new proposals. It is unlikely that all three ingredients will be available in the average school. This is when facilities management can help. The independent expert should be able to identify the

The beginning of the end of the Classroom Register?

school's needs. This will include introducing some lateral thinking, packaging services in an effective manner, and subsequently managing a tendering and negotiating exercise. Key decisions, derived from concise recommendations, will still be made by the client but sound in the knowledge that detailed analysis and expert knowledge have been applied to the task.

Whoever undertakes this work should also put together monitoring routines for continuing contract management. If monitoring and inspection are carried out effectively then standards will be maintained, and significant costs can be saved by triggering non-payment for non-performance. How many heads or school secretaries continue to pass contractors' invoices for payment without challenging them? Once again external support may be crucial to securing contractors and in-house staff performing effectively.

Independence is a key factor. Many experts are in fact linked to a particular contractor and for that reason they should be avoided by all but the most experienced client. It is also, in my view, best to steer clear of those consultants who offer a service for free. They may well negotiate a fee from contractors who are engaged subsequently. Whilst this may be acceptable practice in some quarters, it does not sit comfortably with the usual conventions of managing public funds.

Facilities Management

There is little doubt that the approach outlined in this article to the comprehensive review and redesign of ancillary services does offer potential for schools in the future. Therefore a market for this work is likely to develop and new providers will emerge. In Lincolnshire, the Client Services Group of the Education Department has been pioneering this kind of work, and is now being formed into a Facilities Management Unit. Similar services are likely to be available in other areas, both from LEAs and from private companies.

Objective	— To design and arrange delivery of ancillary services to meet school/college needs effectively and economically.

Starting point	— Gather the data:
	  — current contracts
	  — current costs
	  — performance standards
	  — budget provision.

Key questions for senior school management	— Am I satisfied that all ancillary services are being organised cost effectively and in the style which fits the ethos of this school? — Is there opportunity for moving resources from these services to higher priority tasks or to enhance the contribution made by these services to classroom delivery? — Can further work be done by managers within the school? — Or, do I need outside help?

Table 7.1.2 *Summary checklist for facilities management in schools*

Management and Maintenance of Site and Buildings

Jim Donnelly

The practice of managing the school site will differ for Grant-maintained (GM) schools and those which are under the control of the Local Education Authority (LEA). Since the majority of schools still fall within LEA control, this article deals with them but the important principles of site management apply to all schools; the main difference is that GM schools have wider freedoms – and wider responsibilities. For LEA schools, Local Management of Schools (LMS) changed the old situation where the LEA held the main responsibility for the maintenance of the school buildings – but only up to a point. This is because most schemes of delegation divide the responsibility for the maintenance of buildings between the school (the 'inside') and the LEA (the 'outside'); it is only for those parts which fall within the direct control of the school that there will be money in the school budget.

Responsibilities

The first step in managing the buildings should be to examine the exact nature of the agreement under which the school operates. This will make clear what the school will have to pay for. Examples of the way responsibilities are divided can be seen in the following extracts from one LEA's scheme (see Table 7.2.1).

LEA	SCHOOL
Staircase and landing structures (including handrails and balustrades)	Repairs of finishes and coverings
Servicing, repair and replacement of general electrical installations, including switch gear, cables and conduits up to and including switches, sockets and other outlets	Replacing lamps, tubes, starters and plugs
Heating and domestic hot water distribution systems, including replacement of radiators and other heat emitters, taps and shower fittings	Minor repairs and adjustments to heat emitters, taps and shower fittings

Table 7.2.1 *Division of responsibilities: LEA and individual schools*

It can be readily seen that a dialogue between school and LEA will be necessary at points of overlap. The definition of 'minor repairs', for example, will be critical to the school. If the school wants something done in a hurry it may be necessary to be flexible in one's interpretation.

The interface between LEA and school has already given rise to some interesting issues. For example, in one school the library roof leaked and damaged the floor. The floor was wood-block, covered by carpet. Who should have paid for the repairs? The floor was the LEA's responsibility but was wood-block a floor covering (and hence the school's responsibility) or was it structural (and hence the LEA's)? The matter was further complicated by the fact that the real damage to the carpet was caused not by the rain falling on top of it but by the wood-block expanding underneath it! The LEA was holding central insurance cover for its part but the school had a separate policy for the contents; thus the issue mattered to the insurers and ultimately to the school. In this example, the school paid part of the cost and the LEA paid the rest; however, it could be argued that the school should not have had to pay anything at all. Another school had a large area of the gymnasium floor ruined by leaking heating pipes under the floor. In this case the school insisted that the LEA was responsible for repairing the floor. It can be frustrating waiting for the LEA to carry out the work but a knowledge of one's rights in the matter is important; so is persistence!

Another interesting issue arises over heating systems. It is not illogical to say that the LEA is responsible for the heating system itself (the boilers, controls, etc) and that the school is responsible for paying for fuel. However, what happens if the governors feel that the system needs replacing, either because it is beyond its useful life or because it uses a fuel (eg oil) which is costing more than another fuel (eg gas) would? At present, the school has to try to persuade the LEA that it would be worth changing the system. However, there is no financial incentive for the LEA to do this unless they reach an agreement with the governors that the first savings will be used to pay for a change to the system.

The scheme in Table 7.2.1 makes the LEA responsible for all electrical sockets and switches. What happens if a socket is dangerous – or if the school thinks it is? This is where the LEA needs to be very prompt in dealing with the matter. It is not an option for a school to allow students (or staff) to be near dangerous sockets. You need to be very clear whether the LEA allows for emergency electrical work to be done – and who can authorise it. Schools cannot wait for LEA officers to come from leave to deal with such things!

Working with the LEA

These examples indicate that it is absolutely essential to establish as clearly as possible where the demarcation lines are drawn: be clear what the school budget is for. The next stage is to find out what the LEA plans to spend on the outside of the buildings. Ask to meet the maintenance officer and try to get some answers about where his/her priorities lie for your school for the next year and beyond. Try to ensure that such priorities tie in with the school's, if necessary by bargaining. It is essential that governors (including LEA nominees) are involved in this process. If it seems necessary, confirm any promises in writing. If you have a governors' sub-committee, it is a very good idea to take them round the building in daylight so that they know at first hand what they are talking about. If you can get senior LEA officers (and local councillors) to make similar tours, so much the better! Sometimes they have no idea of the state of the building since they have little, if any, day-to-day contact with it.

The school maintenance budget

Having ascertained where the school's responsibilities lie, it is necessary for the governors to plan a maintenance programme. The first thing is *not* to decide how to spend the money but instead to turn to the school's mission statement and/or school development plan (SDP), and see whether it is expressed in these terms or not. (LMS is about management, *not* about money.) It is important to be as farsighted as one can about curricular needs in the future since this will dictate how rooms and other areas are to be used. The SDP is also likely to include a mention of the environment in which staff and students are to work. These are important parameters in identifying priorities for expenditure under any budget heading, and none more so than here. Many governing bodies delegate the responsibility for the maintenance budget to a sub-committee. The sub-committee can then set out its priorities, preferably for more than one year. Every school will have its own order of priority; Table 7.2.2 indicates how an annual priority list can be set out.

---

1. Removal of all graffiti, both internal and external, as soon as it appears.
2. Immediate repair of broken windows and damaged doors.
3. Improvement of student facilities (eg toilets, showers)
4. Maintenance of appearance of all 'public' areas (for example, the entrance hall).
5. Refurbishment within technology and PE faculties, in consultation with the staff concerned.

Table 7.2.2 *Maintenance priorities of 'this school' 1994/95*

This simple priority list is then used when requests for expenditure are made. The senior staff have a clear rationale for any decisions, with the authority to act right away when vandalism occurs. Some schools are already finding that it is sensible to look at the items under 3, 4 and 5 later in the financial year when the needs under 1 and 2 are clearer.

Staff need to be aware of the policy. They will find it easier to cope with less than ideal surroundings if they know that at least there are plans to ameliorate them to some degree in the future. If they are involved in setting priorities – as suggested in the example above – this will have a beneficial effect on morale. Students should also be aware of their importance in maintaining pleasant working conditions. Schools with positive policies in this area find that, for example, graffiti in the school is much reduced, at least inside the building.

There needs to be a clear understanding within the school of where responsibility for decision-making lies. Obviously the total budget for maintenance will have been set by the governors and guidelines such as those suggested above may exist. However, it also needs to be clear who can authorise this expenditure. It is the head, or a nominated deputy, or the caretaker? Who do staff inform about broken windows or graffiti? How do staff have an input into the planning of the expenditure on improvements?

Procedures

For items of expenditure in excess of certain sums, the LEA financial regulations are likely to indicate particular procedures. For example, there may be a requirement that two or more quotations are obtained for work in excess of a certain amount (a wise move in any case) and there may be a list of approved contractors.

In some schools, a noticeable result of LMS has been the appointment of a part-time handyman or a caretaker/handyman, who can undertake minor improvements. If this is contemplated, one needs to be very clear about the implications for financial control (one cannot just hand a caretaker £20 out of one's back pocket!) and legal responsibility (both towards the employee and anyone who is hurt as a result of negligent workmanship). One needs to examine these issues very carefully *before* any problems arise; it is likely to be too late afterwards.

If your LEA maintenance officer is not proactive in checking your buildings regularly, then a lot of caretaker/head/deputy head time

Portakabin®

Building Solutions for Schools

can be taken up in doing what is really not their job. If this happens, then questions need to be asked about the bit of the LEA budget which is paying for the maintenance officer's salary.

Grounds' maintenance

One aspect of site management which needs particular mention is grounds' maintenance. There are rules set out by the government relating to what is known as Compulsory Competitive Tendering (CCT). These rules exist mainly to ensure that local authorities open all aspects of their work to market forces. Although not designed to set out how schools operate, they do impinge upon a number of areas of school management, including grounds' maintenance. A school has three main choices: it can have the LEA manage the contract, employ its own grounds' maintenance staff or put the contract out to tender.

There are four particular points to note about grounds' maintenance. First, it is not disastrous if the grass is not cut for one week. Second, it is not always possible to decide how often the grass will need to be cut (compare your own efforts in the garden during the recent wet summers with the drier ones!). Third, you may wish to cover your legal responsibilities for controlling litter by including it in the contract. Finally, it is possible to make savings on grounds' maintenance by cutting back on what you specify.

It is important to remember that the school should have a policy on what the grounds will look like, subject to budgetary constraints. Start with the ideal, cost each part of it and then prioritise. It is important that the PE staff in particular are involved in this process since they more than anyone else will find curriculum delivery difficult if the pitches and other sports' facilities are not properly maintained. As far as possible specify exactly what has to be done. If, for example, you specify that the litter must be cleared totally each week – and you have asked for an itemised contract bid – then you can deduct money from the next invoice if it has not been done. The experience of schools which have opted to put their grounds' maintenance contract out to tender is that they have gained much more control over how the school looks and in a lot of cases have saved money as well.

Finally, a summary of advice on maintenance of buildings, based on experience of LMS so far would be:

Management and Maintenance

1. Be persistent.

2. Have regard to the school's aims and school development plan.

3. Involve governors and staff.

4. Plan in advance.

5. Produce written policy on priorities.

6. Make staff roles clear.

7. Involve students in the care of the school.

8. Be persistent!

Managing Learning Resources

Danny Lewis

Introduction

This chapter focuses on policy and planning for the learning
resources service in a secondary school. The service aims to promote
resource-based learning and is responsible for organising library
and resource areas and audio-visual aids, and the design and
printing of materials and information technology (IT). The latter
will only be briefly considered as it is the subject of the next chapter.

Should the learning resources service include all these functions?
Although they could be managed separately there are common
concerns between them, such as resource-based learning, and there
needs to be school-wide consistency and coherence in policy and
practice in the use of resources. Also, new technology, such as desktop publishing and CD-ROM, is blurring traditional distinctions in
resource management, requiring roles to be more flexible over a
range of activities.

Models for policy and planning

The general aim of the service is to support pupils in their learning
and staff in the delivery of the curriculum. An emphasis on
resource-based learning should allow pupils to become more
independent and able to use a wide range of resources. Six
principles may be identified for policy and planning:

- supporting the aims of the school;

- using high-quality resources;
- setting up clear procedures based on economy, efficiency and effectiveness;
- ensuring staff participation and development;
- implementing a broad equal opportunities perspective;
- fully utilising ideas and help from people outside the school.

These principles can be used to set up models of good practice for each aspect of the learning resources service, from which can come more precise objectives, issues for discussion, criteria for evaluating effectiveness and plans for action.

The Open University has suggested five stages for looking at resources in schools (Open University, 1988):

- *mobilisation* involves identifying and providing resources, such as the funding for a library;
- *allocation* is about spending the money and, for example, distributing equipment (like the location of your network rooms);
- *utilisation* is using the resources;
- *control* is developing systems to check the use of resources eg setting up procedures for recording resources on a database, security, health and safety, loan and retrieval, charging, copyright control and repairs;
- *review* is the evaluation of the use of resources.

OFSTED inspections will look at the availability, accessibility, quality and efficient use of resources. Where provision is good, there will be a wide range of effective and appropriate resources with equality of access for all pupils, enabling them to work independently and collaboratively, both for reference purposes and enjoyment. Inspection teams will ascertain whether there are undue pressures on central, shared resources and whether working practices are safe. They will be looking to see if there is a wasteful replication of resources, especially where there is no central inventory to inform staff of what is available. They will check that resources such as educational broadcasts have been audited and their use monitored. Resources are seen as unsatisfactory where they are insufficient, inappropriate, ignored or inaccessible.

Applying the principles and stages

Using these principles, stages and guidelines, we can look at an example of policy and planning for a good library. It would be well stocked with a range of high-quality materials reflecting equal opportunities, and would be used for general reading, loans and study throughout the school day. Equipment and furniture would be in good condition and there would be displays on the walls. There would be full-time paid supervision and additional help from staff, pupils and parents. The atmosphere would be purposeful and the security good. There would be an effective loan and retrieval system and the librarian would have a range of monitoring procedures to help review effectiveness. Information technology would be well used and might include a database and loan system, CD-ROM and Campus 2000. The librarian would consult staff about the purchase of stock and use of the library and develop links with people and organisations outside the school. Occasionally, special events would be set up and guest speakers invited to raise the profile of the library.

Each of the points above could then be examined in more detail. A well-stocked library, for example, probably means about ten books per pupil, with a minimum of 35 per cent fiction. Funding needs to be about £5 to £6 per pupil. Useful comparative data is provided by school library publications, services, advisers and other schools and sets a regional/national context for the library. This may lead to a request for better funding, which can be backed up by research. An analysis can then be made of other aspects of the library to see how well it is doing and make suggestions for the future. The Devon County Council publication *Resources For Learning* is a good guide for this kind of evaluation.

This review may lead to areas of controversy that need to be discussed and resolved. An example of this is the development of satellite resource centres. A large central resource area with a full range of facilities is more economical, efficient and effective because staff and resources are used to help the whole school. Departments, though, may want to set up their own resource areas nearer to their classrooms. It seems reasonable to ensure that the main library or resource area is adequately funded with full-time supervision before spending extra money on satellite centres, which, in principle, are a good idea provided the department can keep stock secure. If the main library is too small and cannot be enlarged then it may be appropriate to set up a second supervised resource area. If satellite centres are developed then it would help to have all the resources listed on a networked database accessible from any area (Kingham, 1993).

Turning policy into practice

Resource-based learning

Sometimes a review of learning resources may raise issues where the objective is relatively clear but the means of achieving it are more difficult. An example is the desire for a school to develop good resource-based learning. The standard text on the subject is by Beswick (1977), still a good read despite its age. A more recent publication covering similar ground is *A Devon Approach to Learning Through Resources*. Good practice would see pupils coming to a library resource area with a clear purpose and able to extract information from a range of sources. Poor practice would see pupils copying large chunks of print from one source. Resources staff can give practical help in the library and perhaps in library skills lessons, but this is insufficient. The deeper issue is cross-curricular and has to involve the whole school, with support from senior management, wide-ranging discussions, and departments willing to clarify precisely how their activities can help to support the development of study skills.

Audio-visual aids

With audio-visual aids, the learning resources service should hold centrally a full range of equipment available on loan. Where departments are allowed to buy items, there should be a school policy to deal with what is purchased, lending arrangements and repairs. Proposals for major purchases should be discussed with a senior member of staff (eg the Head of Learning Resources). There should be regular safety checks on all equipment. TV programmes should be recorded by learning resources so that a central record of what is available can be established. Departments may, of course, want to keep their own stock of recordings. The aim is to achieve a successful relationship between central and departmental control of equipment with respect to purchase, storage, accessibility, and costs of repairs.

Printing

Good practice in the design and printing of materials would emphasise high-quality production, using the latest information technology, including desk-top publishing and laser printing. Colour facilities are now available for desktop publishing and laser printing, but the costs may be inhibitive. The decision about which printing method to use depends on existing equipment, finance available, the cost per sheet (including estimated labour costs) and the facilities needed. Particular care and objective advice are needed when entering into leasing agreements with suppliers of photocopiers. The printing service should be efficient with a short turn-around, certainly within one week, plus an emergency back-up service. Departments may be charged for work done at roughly average cost price, although higher charges may be necessary for peripheral photocopiers to discourage long runs. PIN numbers or photocopy cards can be used to record staff use. Key requirements are quality of output, the best available method for printing and rigour in meeting deadlines.

Staffing

A final consideration is the role of staff in delivering a learning resources service of high quality. Studies of non-teaching support staff show that their work is characterised by its high volume, pace and pressure, the latter increasing when there are excessive interruptions, peaking of duties, insufficient staff and poor organisation. Role conflict and stress can often occur, and the frequent lack of promotion prospects means that job satisfaction must be nurtured in other ways. Training is important because it enables staff to become more skilled and take on new challenges. Job descriptions need to be clear but broad enough to allow for changing needs. Delegation of responsibility encourages a professional approach to work although there must be regular meetings of service staff to monitor progress and plan future targets. When changes take place or conflicts arise, extra time should be arranged for discussion with the line manager (eg Head of Learning Resources). There should be regular meetings of a Learning Resources Committee with representatives for all major departments and key support staff such as the librarian and resources technician. The Head of Learning Resources needs direct contact with senior management to ensure this area is fully considered during whole-school planning.

Conclusion

From the effective translation of learning resources policy into practice should emerge essential documents including a policy statement, a staff learning resources handbook and short and long-term planning documents. Priorities for action can be determined and reviewed each half-term to avoid emphasis on day-to-day needs.

With a clear understanding of the principles for organising and implementing a Learning Resources policy, the school can effectively manage the impact of recent developments, especially the National Curriculum, new inspection procedures and changing technology.

References and further reading

Beswick, N (1977), *Resource-Based Learning*, Heinemann.
Devon County Council (1990) *A Devon Approach to Learning Through Resources*.
Devon County Council (1990) *Resources For Learning*.
HMI (1989) *Better Libraries, Good Practice in Schools*, HMSO.
Kingham, P (1993) *Clearing the Cobwebs, Managing Schools Today*, Vol 2 No 8.
OFSTED (1993) *Handbook for the Inspection of Schools*, HMSO.
Open University (1988) *Managing School Resources, Managing Schools*, Block 5.

Information Technology: Policy and Planning

Andre Wagstaff

Wise tales

> *A forest fire swept towards the river; caught in its path, a squirrel appealed for help to an owl sitting in the same tree. The owl mused a while and then advised 'Fly across the river, squirrel. For fire cannot cross water, and you will be safe.' 'Thanks,' said the squirrel, 'but the problem is – I cannot swim and have no wings. How then can I cross the river?' The owl barely blinked. 'Oh,' he said easily. 'I have given you the broad strategy. You're now asking about implementation, and we owls leave **that** to others'.*

The fable encapsulates both the role and dilemma of senior management when facing the task of developing the use of IT in the school. Undoubtedly the broad stategy within an institution has to be drawn up by senior management – but that must be based upon some knowledge of how IT can be used. (And at this point you might well demand to know if this article will conclude with a ringing appeal for senior managers to buckle down to courses in C++ computer programming. On the contrary, you would be well advised to ignore any such advice.) What, then, can be done?

Here are two cautionary stories. First, make sure the senior management team acquire some experience of IT. Fifteen years ago I visited a large multi-national corporation. Nine-tenths of the organisation reflected all the sterotypes of big business. Earnest looking managers in subdued suits drew up, implemented and monitored policies of impeccable logic and coherence. Through a pass-key-controlled door lay the Data Processing Department. It was full of laid-back characters with designer stubble and a cavalier attitude to anything except playing Dungeons and Dragons on the mainframe. This crew was 'managed' by one of the suited gentlemen, who had never visited their department, found computers essentially a distasteful development, and had delegated all decision-making to the 'techies'. The collapse of the corporation cannot be entirely laid at the door of this abdication of managerial responsibility – but it was a most significant ingredient.

Second, remember that technology is moving very quickly, and whatever you buy now will need to be upgraded or replaced. Ten years ago, I attended meeting where an expert demonstrated the range of machines available to schools. After the presentation, one of the heads came up to the presenter. 'We have decided to buy this model of computer, is that a wise choice?' The presenter gave total reassurance but absolutely no guarantees. 'Thanks for that,' said the head, walking off. 'You see, we were scared stiff of being stuck with the wrong machine for the next 25 years'. Well, predictions are scary things to make, but we know enough about IT to be able to guarantee that noboby will ever be stuck with the wrong machine for 25 years because the technology is moving so fast.

Friendly advice

Perhaps the best advice is to concentrate upon the human dimensions of the issue. Essentially there are fewer than six groups involved:

- senior managers;
- line managers;
- consultants/advisers;
- computer manufacturers;
- software developers; and
- end-users (teaching and non-teaching staff, and learners).

Each group has its own set of aims and objectives. If senior management is to have any chance of fostering the development and implementation of any meaningful strategy for IT, then it needs to understand the factors driving each of these groups.

Senior management is driven by the need to control and shape

OKI

People to People Technology

Technology of Tomorrow

When you buy an OKI product, you're not just buying one of the most advanced products in the world, you're buying into a company with over 110 years of history and a commitment to the future. Through the most comprehensive R&D resources, OKI will always strive to offer unrivalled standards both in products and in service.

OKI is one of the world's top three printer manufacturers, with a group turnover in excess of £2.6 billion. Over 5.5 million people use OKI dot matrix and page printers worldwide, and OKI is the second largest manufacturer and supplier of printer engines to the page printer market.

OKI now also manufacture fax products and was the first company in the world to develop the fax commercially – OKIFAX thermal and plain paper fax machines are working today in almost every country across the globe.

OKIFAX

All OKIFAX products are easy to set up and simple to operate, yet are packed with features that ensure sending documents and information along the telephone line is fast and reliable.

OKI provides plain paper and thermal faxes, starting with the lightweight, slimline desktop thermal OKIFAX 450, ideal for home and business use. This fax provides paper cutter, one touch and dialling, voice assisted auto switching for fax and telephone and remote activated reception.

The OKIFAX 1000 is a popular product, being economical, yet sophisticated – an entry level plain paper fax and copier for the business user. With all the benefits of OKI's new LED page printer, the OKIFAX 1000 delivers excellent print quality and low running costs. Top quality features include 32 greyscale printing, very compact design, fast transmission at only 10 seconds per page and, one touch, coded, chain dialling and broadcast transmission. And, as an added bonus, the OKIFAX 1000 will also provide up to 99 copies at a time.

OKI's top of the range OKIFAX product is the OKIFAX 2300, a powerful, high speed departmental plain paper product capable of broadcast transmission to 120 locations, with full memory facilities.

DOC. IT

DOC.IT – it's a printer, a fax, a scanner, a copier all in one unit.

Amongst the OKI range of products is the DOC.IT, launched in July 1993, the only document processing document that has succeeded in integrating industry, standard office software with scanning, photocopying and faxing all in one single desktop unit.

DOC.IT features DOC.IT Manager, a sophisticated Windows based software manager and graphical user interface that lets you easily intput, process, output and communicate information right at your desktop. DOC.IT greatly increases the productivity of your work.

Prices start from around £3295 RRP.

Page Printers

The Oki page printers use state-of-the-art technology and are capable of reproducing graphics and an almost infinite variety of fonts superbly. They are quiet, efficient and highly reliable. Through the use of separate toner and drum, they offer significant savings on running costs. OKI's commitment to quality is demonstrated by being approved to BS5750.

Un-
believably
it's a fax, a scanner,
a printer
and a copier.

(Unsurprisingly it's an OKI.)

❝ The OKI DOC•IT has no rivals.
It is unique. Not only is it a desktop
document processor from which you can
produce graphics, scan images, edit
complicated text, take copies, it is
also a plain paper fax. By combining
essential office equipment at your desk,
DOC•IT improves your productivity.
You can enter text or pictures directly,
or even remotely using a fax, combine
them in Windows* and then print or fax
the result. And because we use OKI
technology DOC•IT will improve the
quality of your presentation. In fact,
all the hardware and software on the
DOC•IT are totally integrated. And as
it has been produced in conjunction with
Microsoft,* it is Windows* compatible.
So whatever you need to do, you'll
find the OKI DOC•IT does it with
less fuss, less mess, and less waste.
Solutions available from £3,295 RRP.
Call now on **0800 525585**. It won't take
a minute, yet it will save you hours. ❞

OKI
People to People Technology

the direction, attitudes and relationships of the whole organisation. What they must realise is that IT, by its nature, changes the ways in which systems and people interrelate. They must also understand that change, when properly controlled and planned, can often be beneficial.

Line managers often take responsibility for the detailed implementation of an IT policy. Some line managers are ambitious and seek success to further enhance their career prospects. Some measure their worth to an organisation in terms of the size of budget or number of staff they control. Senior management will need to offer every encouragement to them to become open about mistakes and failures, to view their peers as fellow collaborators rather than competitors for scarce resources. Above all, line managers should be guided towards shouldering responsibility, and not be content to simply act as a conduit for exchanging pressures from above and below.

Most senior managers will wish, at some stage, to seek external advice when drawing up an IT strategy. Today there is a wide range available. But be aware that many have a bias – some towards particular brands or types of technology, some to particular methodologies. So how can senior management ensure that they get the best external advice? Begin by listening to the opinions of those who have already been advised. Never hesitate to take up references or visit other schools.

Choosing hardware and software

Hardware manufacturers are facing difficult times. Time was when they could choose between being small volume sellers at high retail margins, or trading in huge quantities at lower profits per unit sold. Sometimes the pattern was to begin small and then lower the sales price as volume of demand increased. Today, the markets have become nearer to those of commodities. You cannot really be a small player and survive for long. Product life cycles are now measured in months rather than years. All this means that manufacturers cannot, dare not, take those long term views so necessary in education.

So senior managers should draw up strategies based on availability, price and functionality over a period of say, three or four years.

Software developers have learned three important lessons. First, they know that it is the software which really sells IT to the potential customer. Second, the price people will pay for the

Get the facts on IT
●●●●●●●●●●●●●●●●

The role of the head teacher is vital in ensuring an information technology (IT) system for the whole school.

But achieving this may seem daunting. Head teachers who have taken the plunge advise:

- **put IT investment in the context of the vision for the whole school**
- **allocate resources**
- **consult with staff**
- **ask manufacturers and sales people the right questions**
- **allow a trial period.**

To help head teachers achieve their IT goals, NCET has produced a series of three information sheets entitled 'Investing in Information Technology Guidelines' – N° 1 'Choosing software and hardware', N° 2 'Formulating a plan' and N° 3 'Financial issues'. These are available free of charge from: *The Information Officer, NCET, Milburn Hill Road, Science Park, Coventry CV4 7JJ. Telephone: 0203 416994*

NCET develops and promotes the use of technology in every area of education and training.

●●●●●●●
The National Council for Educational Technology is a registered charity funded by the Department for Education to be the national focus of expertise in educational technology.
●●●●●●●●

software is directly geared to the market price of the hardware. Ten years ago the kind of word processor available on a high-end computer network would have cost you perhaps £5,000. Today, it may well be sold as part of a software bundle for a twentieth of that. Third, it is the upgrades which really earn the money. I am writing this on version 5 of a word processor. Now I'm very sure that everything I've done could have been accomplished using version 1 – but not certain. And that's the hook that drives the customer down the upgrade path. Add these three lessons together and the result is massive advertising campaigns for software, in which the application with the most features is (on the Swiss Army knife model) the best buy. The initial price may be attractive, but the upgrades will come thick and fast.

Senior managers need to be aware that someone, somewhere out there has problems just like theirs. And if there are enough of them (and there usually are), then developers will have created a range of software to solve these problems. So any claim to being the unique solution should be viewed with some suspicion. It implies that either the problem is unique (and how many truly unique problems are there?), or more likely, that the developer is early to market (and do you really want to be used as a guinea pig?). A salutory lesson learned by one LEA was the choice they made of Management

Information Systems software. Only three other LEAs in the country chose to use it. The consequence was horrifically expensive upgrades, and in the face of this, they had to withdraw it despite its technical advantages.

Senior management also needs to be aware of the concerns of the end-user, says, a teacher who may see IT simply as something that helps get the job done. No more, no less. And if it doesn't work, first time 'right out of the box', then it could be judged part of the problem and not a solution. Any implementation strategy needs to include careful planning to ensure that the introduction of IT into the work patterns of the end-user is effected in the most non-threatening and supportive manner possible. Many strategies fail because they offer benefits to the organisation without providing any payoffs to the individuals actually expected to directly engage with the technology.

One final thought

It is easy to add up the costs of the hardware and the software. It is even possible to make a fair stab at costing the maintenance of it all. Really far-seeing management makes allowance for ultimate replacement. But excellent management goes one step further, because it knows that this sum, however huge, is like the sprinkling of chocolate on a cappuccino. It is a total waste unless what lies beneath is of equal quality. We often forget that getting value out of this equipment and software is predicated on its use by people. So excellent management places an overarching emphasis on staff development, support and training. Because excellent management knows that IT is only as good as the people who use it. And the management of those people is at the heart ot excellent management.

Information Technology: Implementation

Margaret Bell

Effective use of information technology (IT) enhances learning and streamlines administration work

In virtually every school I have seen, the level of IT success has depended on the commitment of the senior management team.

'When I see youngsters getting onto the CD-ROM (Compact Disc – Read Only Memory) or the interactive video, calling up whatever they need for themselves, then I feel we have succeeded', says Peter MacDonald-Pearce, principal at Uppingham Community College in Leicestershire. He feels that learner independence is enhanced through using interactive technology like CD-ROM.

'You see the children coming in during their lunch break, really enjoying what they are doing. It has opened my eyes, and I'm trying to do more,' he said.

Carole Pearce, former head of Ravensdale Infant School in Coventry, argues that the whole process must be mangement-led, involving staff in identifying the IT needs of the school. 'We have achieved significant learning gains. The four-year-olds cannot wait to get started,' she said.

'We went from individual classroom-based teaching into collaborative teaching across the school. Sitting down together to discuss our collective needs started us working much more closely,' she stressed.

The first step in establishing successful IT practice is deciding

where you want to be in relation to where you are. The matrix below is designed to help headteachers think about the issues involved in planning an IT strategy. This process is always best done through consultation.

Heads and staff should start by asking how IT is already being used. Is it mainly classroom/subject based? Is it used for administration? It may be that your existing systems can simply be upgraded and improved.

Case studies

Consider the case of the Brooksbank School in West Yorkshire. First the senior management team felt there was a need to give IT a high profile within the school. They made a senior teacher responsible for designing an IT policy for the whole school. The policy took into account the need to deliver IT within the National Curriculum and wider needs within the school such as offering vocational courses and building links with industry. The policy was written and agreed after consultation with staff.

This is important in deciding where you want to be. In getting to this point, it helps to assess which equipment and resources will meet your needs. What about maintenance costs? Are there arrangements for support from the dealer if things go wrong? Do staff and students need to be trained?

Training can help build staff confidence. Stuart McLeod, deputy head of Binfield C of E primary school in Berkshire, found that before training was introduced, teachers were uncomfortable with the technology.

'Those individuals who were confident enough to try, were investing their own time after school,' he recalls. 'In the main, the two of us who were most confident did a lot of troubleshooting. But it became inefficient for the school to have two members of staff running back and forth to sort out quite basic problems.'

The school received support from the local authority and other education bodies to develop a training plan which gave teachers time to sit down and grapple with the school's various computer packages.

At Ellington High School in Ramsgate, IT is used across the curriculum now, but staff became convinced when IT was used as part of staff development. 'Since we've been involved in staff development using interactive video discs, we feel there is more interest on the part of the staff than before. They can see how computer technology can really involve the learner whereas video, for example, tends to be passive,' said Dee Wardley, headteacher.

Peter MacDonald-Pearce feels strongly that staff training is crucial. 'This term we have an INSET programme with the IT coordinator. Each subject area teacher will learn how to use IT in relation to their own area within the National Curriculum. So, the Maths department are working on the requirements for data processing; the Design department is working on graphics. They also combine tasks, so the Design department will also use wordprocessing packages for presenting projects,' he said.

Financing IT

Considering your financial options is an important part of investing in IT. Brooksbank School, for example received £20,000 funding under the Technology in Schools Initiative (TSI) in order to provide industry-standard software and hardware for BTEC courses. Uppingham Community College received funding from the Department of Employment to develop a flexible learning programme. Local education authorities can advise on where to go for help, plus you may want to look into Grants for Education Support and Training (GEST) funding, local business sponsorship, or Parent Teacher Association (PTA) sponsorship.

Although Uppingham Community College has received external funding, Peter MacDonald-Pearce stresses the need for prioritising this investment within the school's own budget. 'If we want to move to making youngsters independent learners, IT investment must be a financial priority,' he stressed.

Common vision

The senior management team should have an 'IT vision', according to John Robinson, headteacher at Howard Primary School in Croydon. 'They should understand the way IT enhances learning and not simply see it as a subject within the National Curriculum,' he said.

IT does have much wider uses. In fact, Brooksbank School's IT policy has five aims:

- to develop pupils' critical awareness of the role IT can play in their lives;
- to develop its use as part of the National Curriculum;
- to ensure continuity and progression; and
- to build on its use in areas where it can enhance learning and to use it as a resource, accessible to all pupils.

From Copier Control to Total Site Management

You'd be surprised how much money is spent on copying. Just check your copier bills for the last year and you'll probably find that copy volume has increased by around 20%. A recent survey suggested that one third of all copies made are unnecessary.

On the other hand users of EMOS Copytex and Copymanager control equipment have found just the opposite – in many cases costs have reduced by 20%.

EMOS control equipment has been used in all education environments to control copying for a number of years. It has a proven track record for cost control which includes selling copies to students and charging back actual usage to departments.

Recently a number of major users of these control systems have sought to expand the use of copier control cards to much broader applications. In particular they want to use the same card (or "Smart Key") for access control, identification and cashless payment systems related to catering, vending and laundries.

EMOS has installed a number of these "Total Site Management Systems" with great success in College and University Campuses – and more will go in during the 1994 summer break. A single token – a plastic chip or magnetic stripe card or a "smart key" which identifies the individual and carries "cash" is the key element of the system.

What are the school's aims?

- to incorporate IT into subject areas?
- and improve performance in those areas?
- to develop flexible learning?
- to set up an automated management information system?

What are the school's resources?

- staff skills?
- staff time?
- what equipment is there?
- how much space?

What sources of finance are available?

- capitation?
- recurrent grant?
- GEST funding?
- PTA sponsorship?
- industry sponsorship?
- carryover?

What are the school's options?

- change balance of staff vs resources
- change use of staff
- change balance of curriculum staff vs administration/support staff
- acquire additional staff
- change use of current equipment
- acquire additional equipment

Cost/Benefits

- how will it contribute to achievement of aims and specific objectives?
- meeting requirements of national curriculum?
- how will it contribute to improving the quality of teaching/learning/management?
- by improving staff and/or learners' skills/knowledge/ understanding/performance/ attitude/motivation?
- ability to focus on individual needs?
- more opportunities for independent learning?

Implementation Strategy

Who
- do I need to involve and motivate?
- will take responsibility?
- will train the staff?

What
- training and support will be needed?
- skills will staff/learners need?
- planning and administration will be required?
- equipment will be needed?
- finance will be needed?

Where
- should equipment be located?

When
- should we start?
- should training be given?
- should we review?

How
- should the change be introduced?
- long will we need?
- will required finance be obtained?
- will support of staff be won?
- should training be delivered?

Table 7.5.1 *Planning an IT strategy*

Other heads endorse this approach. John Robinson argues that all staff should be involved and agree on what is being purchased. 'I can't stress enough the particular importance of continuity and progression. If pupils learn to use a mouse in Years 1 and 2, then they should continue to use it in Years 3 and 4,' he said.

Over and over again, headteachers who have invested in IT advise a wide staff consultation exercise and a high-profile role for the IT coordinator.

Final advice

Don't get swept away too quickly. Careful selection of what is on offer and discussions with other schools using similar systems is a good idea.

The benefits of careful planning, consultation and investment can be very worthwhile. Peter MacDonald Pears says: 'Once the children get the bit between their teeth and become confident, they will lead the way.'

In order to help senior managers plan this process, NCET has produced a set of three information sheets: 1 'choosing software and hardware', 2 'formulating a plan' and 3 'financial issues'. These are available free of charge from The Information Officer, NCET, Milburn Hill Road, Science Park, Coventry, CV4 7JJ. Tel: 0203 416994.

Part Eight

Useful Addresses and Directory of Products and Services

Useful Names and Addresses

Advisory Conciliation and Arbitration Service (ACAS), Clifton House, 83–117 Euston Road, London NW1 2RB Tel: 071 396 5100.

Advisory Unit: Computers in Education, 126 Great North Road, Hatfield, Herts AL9 5JZ Tel: 0707 266714

Association of Graduate Careers Advisory Services, c/o Careers Advisory Services, University of Central Lancashire, Preston, PR1 2TQ Tel: 0772 892580

Association of Heads of Independent Schools (AHIS), Abbott's Hill School, Bunkers Lane, Hemel Hempstead, Herts HP3 8RP Tel: 0442 403333

Association for Language Learning, 16 Regent Place, Rugby, Warwickshire CV21 2PN Tel: 0788 546443

Association of Teachers and Lecturers (ATL), 7 Northumberland Street, London WC2N 5DA Tel: 071 930 6441

British Educational Equipment Association, 20 Beaufort Court, Admiral's Way, London E14 9XL Tel: 071 537 4997

British Educational Management and Administration Society (BEMAS), Contact: Professor L E Watson, Sheffield Hallam University, 36 Collegiate Crescent, Shefield S10 2BP Tel: 0742 720911

British Standards Institute, Linford Wood, Milton Keynes, MK14 6LE Tel: 0908 21166

Business and Technology Education Council (BTEC), Central House, Upper Woburn Place, London WC1H 0HH Tel: 071 413 8400

Central Bureau for Educational Visits and Exchanges, Seymour Mews House, Seymour Mews, London W1H 9PE Tel: 071 486 5101

Centre for Information on Language Teaching and Research, 20 Bedfordbury, London WC2N 4LB Tel: 071 379 5101

Chartered Institute of Public Finance and Accountancy (CIPFA), 3 Robert Street, London WC2N 6BH Tel: 071 930 3456

City and Guilds London Institute, 46 Brittania Street, London WC1X 9RG Tel: 071 278 2468

College of Preceptors, Coppice Row, Theydon Bois, Epping, Essex CM16 7DN Tel: 0992 812727

School Management Handbook

Commission of the European Communities, 8 Storey's Gate, London SW1P 3AT Tel: 071 973 1992

Commission for Racial Equality, Elliot House, 10–12 Allington Street, London SW1E 5EH Tel: 071 828 7022

Council of Local Education Authorities (CLEA), Eaton House, 66A Eaton Square, London SW1W 9BH Tel: 071 235 1200

Department for Education Publications' Despatch Centre, Honeypot Lane, Cannons Park, Stanmore, Middlesex HA7 1AZ

'Education Matters' Radio 5 programme on educational issues. Contact: 'Education Matters', Broadcasting House, Portland Place, London W1A 4WW Tel: 071 580 4468

Education Partners Overseas, Contact: Jean Burroughs, EPO, 1 Catton Street, London WC1R 4AB Tel: 071 831 4013

Equal Opportunities Commission, Overseas House, Quay Street, Manchester M3 3HN Tel: 061 833 9244

European Cultural Foundation, Pilgrims, Appledore, Nr Ashford, Kent TN26 2AE Tel: 023383 215

European Movement, 158 Buckingham Palace Road, London SW1W 9TR Tel: 071 824 8388

European Secondary Heads Association, Contact: Henk Oonk, c/o CEVNO, Nassauplein 8, 1815 GM Alkmaar, The Netherlands Tel: 010 31 72 11 85 02

Exchange of Commonwealth Teachers, Contact: Miss Jean Thompson, 7 Lion Yard, Tremadoc Road, Clapham, London SW4 7NQ Tel: 071 498 1101

Grant-Maintained Schools Centre, The Wesley Court, 4a Priory Road, High Wycombe, Bucks HP13 6SE Tel: 0494 474470

Health Education Authority, Hamilton House, Mabledon Place, London WC1H 9TX Tel: 071 383 3833

Health and Safety Commission, Baynards House, 1 Chepstow Place, Westbourne Grove, London W2 4TF Tel: 071 243 6000

Health and Safety Executive (HSE), St Hugh's House, Stanley Precinct, Bootle L20 3QY Tel: 051 951 4000

In-Service Staff Tutors Associations, North Riding College, Filey Road, Scarborough, N Yorks YO11 3AZ Tel: 0723 362392

Industrial Society, 3 Carlton House Terrace, London SW1Y 5AF Tel: 071 839 4300

The International Confederation of Principles, Contact: Dr Tim Dyer, c/o NASSP, 1904 Association Drive, Reston, Virginia 22091–1537, USA Tel: 0101 703 860 0200

Local Government International Bureau, 35 Great Smith Street, London SW1P 3BJ Tel: 071 222 1636

Mediascene Ltd, PO Box 90, Hengoed, Mid Glamorgan CF8 9YE

National Association of Governors and Managers, 21 Bennetts Hill, Birmingham B2 5QP Tel: 021 643 5787

National Association of Headteachers, 1 Heath Square, Boltro Road, Haywards Heath, West Sussex RH16 1BL Tel: 0444 458133

National Association of Inspectors and Educational Advisers, 1 Heath Square, Boltro Road, Haywards Heath, West Sussex RH16 1BL Tel: 0444 441279

268

Useful Names and Addresses

National Confederation of Parent-Teacher Associations, 2 Ebbsfleet Industrial Estate, Stonebridge Road, Gravesend, Kent DA11 9DZ

National Educational Resources Information Service, Maryland College, Leighton Street, Woburn, Milton Keynes MK17 9JD Tel: 0525 290364

National Foundation for Educational Research, The Mere, Upton Park, Slough SL1 2DQ Tel: 0753 574123

National School Curriculum Assessment Authority, Newcombe House, 45 Notting Hill Gate, London W11 3JB Tel: 071 229 1234

The Open University, Central Enquiry Service, PO Box 200, Milton Keynes MK7 6YZ Tel: 0908 653231

The Professional Association of Teachers, 2 St James Court, Friar Gate, Derby DE1 1BT Tel: 0332 372337

RSA Examinations Board, Westwood Way, Coventry, CV4 8HS Tel: 0203 470033

School Library Association, Liden Library, Barrington Close, Lidon, Swindon SN3 6HF Tel: 0793 617838

School Management South, Professional Centre, Furnace Drive, Furnace Green, Crawley, West Sussex RH10 6JB

Secondary Heads Association, 130 Regent Road, Leicester LE1 7PG Tel: 0533 471797

Society of Education Officers (SEO), 20 Bedford Way, London WC1H 0AP Tel: 071 323 0029

Special Educational Needs – National Advisory Council, Department of Education, The University, Liverpool L69 3BX Tel; 051 794 2500

Teachers Pension Agency, Department for Education, Mowden Hall, Standrop Road, Darlington, Co Durham DL3 9EE Tel: 0325 460155

UK Centre for European Education, Seymour Mews House, Seymour Mews, London W1H 9PE Tel: 071 486 5101

UK European Parliament Office, 2 Queen Anne's Gate, London SW1H 9AA Tel: 071 222 0411

UK Lingua Unit, Seymour Mews House, Seymour Mews, London W1H 9PE Tel: 071 224 1477

UNISON, Headquarters, 1 Mabledon Place, London WC1H 9AJ Tel: 071 388 2366

University Association for Contemporary European Studies, King's College, Strand, London WC2R 2LS Tel: 071 240 0206

Directory of Products and Services

The headings listed below are those used in the Directory of Products and Services.

Accountancy

Accreditation of learning

Administration

Appraisal systems

Banks

Binding equipment

Books (suppliers)

Carpet/floorcoverings

Cashless catering and vending

Catering services

Cleaning

Cloakroom facilities

Computers, software and systems

Copier control

Curriculum documents

Drama equipment

Educational publishers

Education resources

Electronic registration systems

Energy/facility management

Examining bodies

Furniture

Gymnastic equipment

Heating/ventilation/refrigeration controls

Health and safety

Identification cards/systems

International links

Investors in People – action plans, audits and investment

Laminators

LEA management consultants

Legal advice/services

Lighting

Litter clearance

Management development

Managing staff development

Mobile buildings

National curriculum – planning and delivery

Office supplies and stationery

Pedagogic games and toys

Photographic service

Playground equipment

Professional bodies

Property management

Publications

Seurity – access control, alarms

Special educational needs

Teachers' unions

Training and information

Training consultants and career development

Workshops

Accountancy

Chester Accounting Services Ltd
114–120 Northgate Street
Chester CH1 2HT
Tel: 0244 345525
Fax: 0244 344715

Fraser and Russell
4 London Wall Buildings
Blomfield Street
London EC2M 5NT
Tel: 071 638 3522
Fax: 071 638 9782

Grant Thornton
Grant Thornton House
Melton Street
Euston Square
London NW1 2EP
Tel: 071 728 2742
Fax: 071 383 4334

Kidsons Impey
Spectrum House
20–26 Cursitor Street
London EC4A 1HY
Tel: 071 405 2088
Fax: 071 334 4734

Slater, Chapman and Cooke
16A St James's Street
London SW1A 1ER
Tel: 071 930 7621
Fax: 0071 930 9352

Systems Union Ltd
Northampton Lodge
39A Canonbury Square
London N1 2AN
Tel: 071 354 3131
Fax: 071 354 4599

Accreditation of learning

Centre for Continuing Development
University of Manchester
Oxford Road
Manchester M13 9PL
Tel: 061 275 3463
Fax: 061 275 3519

The National Council for Vocational Qualifications (NCVQ)
222 Euston Road
London NW1 2BZ
Tel: 071 387 9898
Fax: 071 387 0978

Scottish Vocational Education Council (SCOTVEC)
Hanover House
24 Douglas Street
Glasgow G2 7NQ
Tel: 041 248 7900
Fax: 041 242 2244

Administration

Dolphin Computer Services Ltd
5 Mercian Close
Watermoor
Cirencester
Gloucestershire GL7 1LT
Tel: 0285 659291
Fax: 0285 656941

Appraisal systems

Genesis Development International
Viking House
Swallowdale Road
Hemel Hempstead
Hertfordshire HP2 7HA
Tel: 0442 232124
Fax: 0442 232127

Banks

Co-operative Bank Plc
1 Balloon Street
Manchester M60 4EP
Tel: 061 832 3456
Fax: 061 839 8284

Directory of Products and Services

Binding equipment

James Burn International
Douglas Road
Esher
Surrey KT10 8BD
Tel: 0372 466801
Fax: 0372 460151

Books (suppliers)

Books for Students Ltd
Bird Road
Heathcote
Warwick CV34 6TR
Tel: 0926 314366
Fax: 0926 450178

Dillons – The Bookstore
116 New Street
Birmingham B2 4JJ
Tel: 021 631 4333
Fax: 021 643 2441

Dillons – The Bookstore
82 Gower Street
London WC1E 6EG
Tel: 071 636 1577
Fax: 071 580 7680

Letterbox Library
Unit 20
Leroy House
436 Essex Road
London N1 3QP
Tel: 071 226 1633
Fax: 071 226 1768

Somerset Education Services
Somerset County Council
County Hall
Taunton
Somerset TA1 4DY
Tel: 0823 333451
Fax: 0823 338139

Building

Atkins, Lister, Drew Ltd
Woodcote Grove
Ashley Road
Epsom
Surrey KT18 5BW
Tel: 0372 723555
Fax: 0372 743006

Noreast Building Management
Otley Road
Lawnswood
Leeds LS16 5PX
Tel: 0532 303777
Fax: 0532 670394

**PSA Building Management
South & West**
Burghill Road
Westbury on Trym
Bristol BS10 6NH
Tel: 0272 764000
Fax: 0272 764849

Carpets and floorcoverings

Heckmondwike FB Ltd
PO Box 7
Wellington Mills
Liversedge
West Yorkshire WF15 7XA
Tel: 0924 406161
Fax: 0924 409972

We Are Cleaning (GB) Ltd
Midland House
The Avenue
Rubery
Birmingham B45 9AL
Tel: 021 453 6191
Fax: 021 453 9160

Cashless catering and vending

Emos Information Systems
Emos House
2 Treadway Technical Centre
Treadway Hill
High Wycombe
Buckinghamshire HP10 9RS
Tel: 0628 850400
Fax: 0628 850251

Catering services

Cleancare UK Ltd
Mitchell House
333 Bath Street
Glasgow G2 4ER
Tel: 041 331 2848
Fax: 041 221 8517

Compass Services (UK) Ltd
Icknield House
40 West Street
Dunstable
Bedfordshire LU6 1TA
Tel: 0582 600222
Fax: 0582 471180

Cleaning

Cleancare UK Ltd
Mitchell House
333 Bath Street
Glasgow G2 4ER
Tel: 041 331 2848
Fax: 041 221 8517

Paul's Industrial Services Ltd
Edward House
Collingdon Road
Cardiff CF1 5ET
Tel: 0222 498111
Fax: 0222 484775

We Are Cleaning (GB) Ltd
Midland House
The Avenue
Rubery
Birmingham B45 9AL
Tel: 021 453 6191
Fax: 021 453 9160

Cloakroom facilities

We Are Cleaning (GB) Ltd
Midland House
The Avenue
Rubery
Birmingham B45 9AL
Tel: 021 453 6191
Fax: 021 453 9160

Computers, software and systems

Amstrutt
81A West Street
Tavistock
Devon PL19 8AQ
Tel: 0822 610127
Fax: 0822 610127

Campus 2000
Priory House
St John's Lane
London EC1M 4HD
Tel: 071 782 7104
Fax: 071 782 7112

D & E Software Services
Unit 27
Mount Pleasant Industrial Estate
Dep 3
Mount Pleasant Road
Southampton SO2 0SP
Tel: 0703 634120
Fax: 0703 333134

Dolphin Computer Services Ltd
5 Mercian Close
Watermoor
Cirencester
Gloucestershire GL7 1LT
Tel: 0285 659291
Fax: 0285 656941

Indalo Technology Ltd
Apex House
London Road
Bracknell
Berkshire RG12 2TE
Tel: 0344 302344
Fax: 0344 301355

Management Software
MSL House
27 Ackmar Road
London SW6 4UR
Tel: 071 731 7200
Fax: 071 731 8337

Micromail Data Supplies
Ellwood House
5 Kestral Close
Forest Farm
Leicester Forest Gate
LE3 3NN
Tel: 0533 393423
Fax: 0533 393423

NCET
3 Devonshire Street
London NW1 2BA
Tel: 071 636 4186
Fax: 071 636 3798

OKI Systems
550 Dundee Road
Slough Trading Estate
Slough
Berkshire SL1 4LE
Tel: 0753 819819
Fax: 0753 819871

Systems Union Ltd
Northampton Lodge
39A Canonbury Square
London N1 2AN
Tel: 071 354 3131
Fax: 071 354 4599

Whitgift Computer Services
Charterhouse
51–53 Bickersteth Road
London SW1 9SH
Tel: 081 672 2808
Fax: 081 672 2809

Copier control

Emos Information Systems
Emos House
2 Treadway Technical Centre
Treadway Hill
High Wycombe
Buckinghamshire HP10 9RS
Tel: 0628 850400
Fax: 0628 850251

Curriculum documents

**Professional Development
Consultancy**
Hucclecote Centre
Churchdown Lane
Hucclecote
Gloucester GL3 3QN
Tel: 0452 623068
Fax: 0452 623037

Somerset Education Services
Somerset County Council
County Hall
Taunton
Somerset TA1 4DV
Tel: 0823 333451
Fax: 0823 338139

Drama equipment

Lancelyn Theatre Supplies
Poulton Road
Bebington
Wirral L63 9LN
Tel: 051 334 3000
Fax: 051 334 4047

Educational publishers

Cassell Plc
Villiers House
41–47 Strand
London WC2N 5JE
Tel: 071 839 4900
Fax: 071 839 1804

Paul Chapman Publishing Ltd
144 Liverpool Road
London N1 1LA
Tel: 071 609 5315
Fax: 071 609 1057

Collins Educational
Harper Collins
P O Box
Glasgow G4 0NB
Tel: 041 772 3200
Fax: 041 306 3119

Falmer Press Ltd
Rankine Road
Basingstoke
Hampshire RG24 0PR
Tel: 0256 840366
Fax: 0256 479438

HMSO Books
51 Nine Elms Lane
London SW8 5DR
Tel: 071 873 8319
Fax: 071 873 8463

Harcourt Brace Jovanovich Ltd
Foots Cray High Street
Sidcup
Kent DA14 5HT
Tel: 081 300 3322
Fax: 081 309 0807

Hobsons Publishing Plc
Bateman Street
Cambridge CB2 1LZ
Tel: 0223 354551
Fax: 0223 323154

Hodder and Stoughton
Mill Road
Dunton Green
Sevenoaks
Kent TN13 2YA
Tel: 0732 450111
Fax: 0732 460134

Kingscourt Publishing Ltd
London House
271–273 King Street
London W6 9LZ
Tel: 081 741 2533
Fax: 081 741 2292

Kogan Page Ltd
120 Pentonville Road
London N1 9JN
Tel: 071 278 0433
Fax: 071 837 6348

Letts Educational
Aldine House
Aldine Place
London W12 8AW
Tel: 081 740 1111
Fax: 081 740 1184

Longman Group UK Ltd
6th Floor, Westgate House
The High
Harlow
Essex CM20 1YR
Tel: 0279 442601
Fax: 0279 444501

Thomas Nelson and Sons Ltd
Nelson House
Mayfield Road
Walton-on-Thames
Surrey KT12 5PL
Tel: 0932 246133
Fax: 0932 246109

New Education Press Ltd
13 Church Drive
Keyworth
Nottinghamshire NG12 5FG

Open University Press
Celtic Court
22 Ballmoor
Buckingham MK18 1XW
Tel: 0280 823388
Fax: 0280 823233

Oxford University Press
Walton Street
Oxford OX2 6DP
Tel: 0865 56767
Fax: 0865 56646

Publishing and Printing Services Ltd
155–157 Oxford Street
London W1R 1TB
Tel: 071 434 0137
Fax: 071 494 1360

Routledge
11 New Fetter Lane
London EC4P 4EE
Tel: 071 583 9855
Fax: 071 583 0701

Education resources

The Bible Society
Stonehill Green
Westlea
Swindon SN5 7DG
Tel: 0793 513714
Fax: 0793 512539

British Nuclear Fuels Plc
D118
Risley
Warrington WA3 6AS
Tel: 0925 832557
Fax: 0925 833851

Christian Aid
PO Box 100
London SE1 7RT
Tel: 071 620 4444
Fax: 071 620 0719

Duke of Edinburgh's Award
Gulliver House
Madeira Walk
Windsor
Berkshire SL4 1EU
Tel: 0753 810753
Fax: 0753 810666

Health Education Authority
Hamilton House
Mabledon Place
London WC1H 9TX
Tel: 071 383 3833
Fax: 071 387 0500

Hope Education
Orb Mill
Huddersfield Road
Waterhead
Oldham OL4 2ST
Tel: 061 633 6611
Fax: 061 633 3431

Lancashire Education Resources Unit
PO Box 61
County Hall
Fishergate
Preston PR1 8RJ
Tel: 0772 263771
Fax: 0772 263630

Letterbox Library
Unit 20
Leroy House
436 Essex Road
London N1 3QP
Tel: 071 226 1633
Fax: 071 226 1768

The Open College
St Paul's
781 Wilmslow Road
Didsbury
Manchester M20 8RW
Tel: 061 434 0007
Fax: 061 434 1061

RSPCA
Causeway
Horsham
West Sussex RH12 1HG
Tel: 0403 64181
Fax: 0403 41048

Save the Children Education Unit
17 Grove Lane
London SE5 8RD
Tel: 071 703 5400
Fax: 071 703 2278

Somerset Education Services
Somerst County Council
County Hall
Taunton
Somerset TA1 4DV
Tel: 0823 333451
Fax: 0823 338139

UK Atomic Energy Authority
Education Officer
Building 354 West
AERE Harwell
Didcot
Oxfordshire OX11 0RA
Tel/Fax: 0235 821111

UK Nirex Ltd
Curie Avenue
Harwell
Didcot
Oxfordshire OX11 0RH
Tel: 0235 825507
Fax: 0235 821902

Understanding Electricity
Electricity Association Services Ltd
309 Millbank
London SW1P 4RD
Tel: 071 834 2333
Fax: 071 931 0356

Electronic registration systems

Emos Information Systems
Emos House
2 Treadway Technical Centre
Treadway Hill
High Wycombe
Buckinghamshire HP10 9RS
Tel: 0628 850400
Fax: 0628 850251

Mitrefinch Ltd
Mitrefinch House
Trading Estate
Green Lane
Clifton
York YO3 6PY

NBS Ltd
Unit 7
Canada Road
Byfleet Industrial Estate
Byfleet
Weybridge
Surrey KT14 7JL
Tel: 0932 351531
Fax: 0932 351382

Indalo Technology Ltd
Apex House
London Road
Bracknell
Berkshire RG12 2TE
Tel: 0344 302344
Fax: 0344 301355

Real World Services Ltd
3 Sandycroft Close
Birchwood
Warrington
Cheshire WA3 7LY
Tel: 0925 837588

Energy/facility management

CSI World Trade Inc
Building L16
Gyosei International Business Park
London Road
Reading
Berkshire RG1 5AQ
Tel: 0734 756400
Fax: 0734 750897

Drayton Controls (Engineering) Ltd
Chantry Close
West Drayton
Middlesex UB7 7SP
Tel: 0895 444012
Fax: 0895 441288

Examining bodies

Business and Technology Education Council (BTEC)
Central House
Upper Woburn Place
London WC1H 0HH
Tel: 071 413 8400

City and Guilds of London Institute
46 Britannia Street
London WC1X 9RG
Tel: 071 278 3344
Fax: 071 278 9460

Joint Council for the GCSE
8th Floor, Netherton House
23–29 Marsh Street
Bristol BS1 4BP
Tel: 0272 214379

Midland Examining Group
Norfolk House
Smallbrook Queensway
Birmingham B5 4NJ
Tel: 021 631 2151

Northern Examining Association
c/o The Joint Matriculation Board
Manchester M15 6EU
Tel: 061 953 1180
Fax: 061 273 7572

Northern Ireland Schools Examination Council
Beechill House
42 Beechill Road
Belfast BT8 4RS
Tel: 0232 704666
Fax: 0232 799913

Oxford and Cambridge Schools Examination Board
Elsfield Way
Oxford OX2 8EP
Tel: 0865 54421
Fax: 0865 514902
and
Purbeck House
Purbeck Road
Cambridge CB2 2PU
Tel: 0223 411211
Fax: 0223 211501

RSA Examinations Board
Westwood Way
Coventry CV4 8HS
Tel: 0203 470033
Fax: 0203 468080

Scottish Examination Board
Ironmills Road
Dalkeith
Midlothian EH22 1LE

The Southern Examining Group
Central Administration Office
Stag Hill House
Guildford GU2 5XJ
Tel: 0483 503123

**University of London
Examinations and Assessment
Board**
The Lindens
Lexden Road
Colchester
CO3 3RL
Tel: 0206 549595
Fax: 0206 540199

**Welsh Joint Education
Committee**
245 Western Avenue
Cardiff CF5 2YX
Fax: 0222 561231

Furniture

Eibe Play
Forest House
8 Baxter Road
Sale
Cheshire M33 3AL
Tel: 061 962 8295
Fax: 061 962 8295

Gymnastic equipment

Eibe Play
Forest House
8 Baxter Road
Sale
Cheshire M33 3AL
Tel: 061 962 8295
Fax: 061 962 8295

*Heating/ventilation/refrigeration
controls*

**Drayton Controls (Engineering)
Ltd**
Chantry Close
West Drayton
Middlesex UB7 7SP
Tel: 0895 444012
Fax: 0895 441288

Health and safety

**Barleythorpe Management
Resources**
Oakham
Rutland
Leicestershire LE15 7ED
Tel: 0572 723711
Fax: 0572 757657

Noreast Building Management
Otley Road
Lawnswood
Leeds LS16 5PQ
Tel: 0532 303777
Fax: 0532 670394

**PSA Building Management
South & West**
Burghill Road
Westbury on Trym
Bristol BS10 6NH
Tel: 0272 764000
Fax: 0272 764849

**The Royal Society for the
Prevention of Accidents**
Cannon House
The Priory Queensway
Birmingham B4 6BS
Tel: 021 200 2461
Fax: 021 200 1254

Identification cards/systems

Emos Information Systems
Emos House
2 Treadway Technical Centre
Treadway Hill
High Wycombe
Buckinghamshire HP10 9RS
Tel: 0628 850400
Fax: 0628 850251

NBS Ltd
Unit 7
Canada Raod
Byfleet Industrial Estate
Byfleet
Weybridge
Surrey KT14 7JL
Tel: 0932 351531
Fax: 0932 351382

International links

Elwe-Lehr Systeme GmbH
Elwestrasse 6
D-3302 Cremlingen
Germany
Tel: 010 49 5306 7031
Fax: 010 49 5306 7135

Investors in people – action plans, audits and investments

Genesis Development International
Viking House
Swallowdale Road
Hemel Hempstead
Hertfordshire
Tel: 0442 232124
Fax: 0442 232127

Laminators

James Burn International
Douglas Road
Esher
Surrey KT10 8BD
Tel: 0372 466801
Fax: 0372 460151

LEA management consultants

Professional Development Consultancy
Hucclecote Centre
Churchdown Lane
Hucclecote
Gloucester
Tel: 0452 623068
Fax: 0452 623037

Regional Trading Unit
Larkfield High School
Black's Road
Belfast BT10 0NB
Tel: 0232 618121
Fax: 0232 629745

Legal advice/services

Barleythorpe Management Resources
Oakham
Rutland
Leicestershire LE15 7ED
Tel: 0572 723711
Fax: 9572 757651

Collyer-Bristow
4 Bedford Row
London WC1R 4DF
Tel: 071 242 7363
Fax: 071 405 0555

Lighting

GE Lighting Ltd
Miles Road
Mitcham
Surrey CT4 9YX
Tel: 081 640 1221
Fax: 081 640 2842

Litter clearance

Litterpicker
Saint Catherine Valley
Northend
Batheaston
Bath BA1 8ES
Tel: 0225 858093

Management development

Barleythorpe Management Resources
Oakham
Rutland
Leicestershire LE15 7ED
Tel: 0572 723711
Fax: 0572 757651

Centre for Continuing Development
University of Manchester
Oxford Road
Manchester M13 9PL
Tel: 061 275 3463
Fax: 061 275 3519

The Open College
St Paul's
781 Wilmslow Road
Didsbury
Manchester M20 8RW
Tel: 061 434 0007
Fax: 061 434 1061

Professional Development Consultancy
Hucclecote Centre
Churchdown Lane
Hucclecote
Gloucester
Tel: 0452 623068
Fax: 0452 623037

Mobile buildings

Globalmobile Ltd
8 Meadow Lane
Fetcham
Surrey KT22 9UW
Tel: 081 653 3333
Fax: 081 771 2987

Portable Buildings Ltd
Hollygate Industrial Park
Hollygate Lane
Cotgrave
Nottingham NG12 3JW
Tel: 0602 894600
Fax: 0602 892001

Portakabin Ltd
Marketing Services Department
Huntington
York YO3 9PT
Tel: 0904 611655
Telex: 57849 Porta

National curriculum – planning and delivery

Centre for Continuing Development
University of Manchester
Oxford Road
Manchester M13 9PL
Tel: 061 275 3463
Fax: 061 275 3519

Professional Development Consultancy
Hucclecote Centre
Churchdown Lane
Hucclecote
Gloucester
Tel: 0452 623068
Fax: 0452 623037

Timetable Systems
39 Somerset Road
Frome
Somerset BA11 1HD
Tel: 0373 463749
Fax: 0373 452428

Office supplies and stationery

James Burn International
Douglas Road
Esher
Surrey KT10 8BD
Tel: 0372 466801
Fax: 0372 460151

UHU (UK) Ltd
Grove House
551 London Road
Isleworth
Middlesex TW7 4DS
Tel: 081 847 2227
Fax: 081 569 8530

Pedagogic games and toys

Eibe-Play
Forest House
8 Baxter Road
Sale
Cheshire
M33 3AL
Tel: 061 9628295
Fax: 061 9628295

Photographic services

NBS Ltd
Unit 7
Canada Road
Byfleet Industrial Estate
Byfleet
Weybridge
Surrey KT14 7JL
Tel: 0932 351531
Fax: 0932 351382

Playground equipment

Eibe-Play
Forest House
8 Baxter Road
Sale
Cheshire
M33 3AL
Tel: 061 9628295
Fax: 061 9628295

Professional Bodies

Association of Accounting Technicians
154 Clerkenwell Road
London EC1R 5AD
Tel: 071 837 8600
Fax: 071 837 6970

Independent Association of Preparatory Schools

11 Waterloo Place
Leamington Spa
Warwickshire CV32 5LA
Tel: 0926 887883

Institute of Financial Accountants
Burford House
44 London Road
Sevenoaks
Kent TN13 1AS
Tel: 0732 458080
Fax: Fax: 0732 455848

Institute of Training and Development
Marlow House
Institute Road
Marlow
Buckinghamshire SL7 1BD
Tel: 0628 890123
Fax: 0628 890208

The Library Association
7 Ridgmount Street
London WC1E 7AE
Tel: 071 636 7543
Fax: 071 436 7218

Property management

Noreast Building Management
Otley Road
Lawnswood
Leeds LS16 5PQ
Tel: 0532 303777
Fax: 0532 670394

PSA Building Management South & West
Burghill Road
Westbury on Trym
Bristol BS10 6NH
Tel: 0272 764000
Fax: 0272 764849

Publications

**Education Guardian
The Guardian**
119 Farringdon Road
London EC1R 3ER
Tel: 071 278 2332
Fax: 071 837 1267

Professional Development Consultancy
Hucclecote Centre
Churchdown Lane
Hucclecote
Gloucester
Tel: 0452 623068
Fax: 0452 623037

Times Educational Supplement
Priory House
St John's Lane
London EC1M 4BX
Tel: 071 253 3000
Fax: 071 490 0294

Security – access control,
alarms

CSI World Trade Inc
Building L16
Gyosei International Business Park
London Road
Reading
Berkshire RG1 5AQ
Tel: 0734 756400
Fax: 0734 750897

Emos Information Systems
Emos House
2 Treadway Technical Centre
Freadway Hill
High Wycombe
Buckinghamshire HP10 9RS
Tel: 0628 850400
Fax: 0628 850251

Sensormatic Camera Ltd
Rossmore House
Haseley Manor
Hatton
Warwick CV35 7LV
Tel: 0926 484664
Fax: 0926 484454

Special eductional needs

Dyslexia Institute
133 Gresham Road
Staines
Middlesex TW18 2AJ
Tel: 0784 463851
Fax: 0784 460747

Gifted Children's Information
Centre
Hampton Grange
21 Hampton Lane
Solihull B91 2QJ
Tel: 021 705 4547

Learning Development Aids
Duke Street
Wisbech
Cambridgeshire PE13 2AE
Tel: 0945 63441

PLANET (Play Leisure Advice
Network)
c/o Harperbury Hospital
Harper Lane
Shenley
Nr Radlett WD7 9HQ
Tel: 0932 854861

Teachers' unions

Association of Teachers and
Lecturers
7 Northumberland Street
London WC2N 5DA
Tel: 071 930 6441

National Association of Head
Teachers
1 Heath Square
Boltro Road
Haywards Heath
West Sussex RH16 1BL
Tel: 0444 458133
Fax: 0444 416326

NASUWT
Hillscourt Education Centre
Rednal
Birmingham B45 8RS
Tel: 021 453 6150
Fax: 021 453 7224

National Union of Teachers
(NUT)
Hamilton House
Mabledon Place
London WC1H 9BD
Tel: 071 388 6191

The Professional Association of
Teachers
2 St James Court
Friar Gate
Derby DE1 1BT
Tel: 0332 372337
Fax: 0332 290310

Training and information

Action for Governors
Information and Training
AGIT, Community Education
Development Centre
Lyng Hall
Blackberry Lane
Coventry CV2 3JS
Tel: 0203 638660
Fax: 0203 681161

Barleythorpe Management Resources
Oakham
Rutland
Leicestershire
Tel: 0572 723711
Fax: 0572 757657

The Centre for School Effectiveness
Westminster College
North Hinksey
Oxford OX2 9AT
Tel: 0865 245242

Centre for the Study of Comprehensive Schools
The Queen's Building
University of Leicester
Barrack Road
Northampton NN2 6AF
Tel: 0604 24969
Fax: 0604 36326

The College of Preceptors
Coppice Row
Theydon Bois
Essex CM16 7DN
Tel: 0992 812727
Fax: 0992 814690

Dolphin Computer Services Ltd
5 Mercian Close
Watermoor
Cirencester
Gloucestershire GL7 1LT
Tel: 0285 659291
Fax: 0285 656941

Dudley Governor Training
West Docks House
1 Trinity Road
Dudley DY1 1JB
Tel: 0384 452205
Fax: 0384 452216

Dyslexia Institute
133 Gresham Road
Staines
Middlesex TW18 2AJ
Tel: 0784 463851
Fax: 0784 460747

Economic Awareness Teacher Training Programme (EcATT)
University of Manchester
School of Education
Oxford Road
Manchester M13 9PL
Tel: 061 273 4452

Genesis Development International
Viking House
Swallowdale Road
Hemel Hempstead
Hertfordshire HP2 7HA
Tel: 0442 232124
Fax: 0442 232127

Indalo Technology Ltd
Apex House
London Road
Bracknell
Berkshire RG12 2TE
Tel: 0344 302344
Fax: 0344 301355

Institute of Training and Development
Marlow House
Institute Road
Marlow
Buckinghamshire SL7 1BD
Tel: 0628 890123
Fax: 0628 890208

Directory of Products and Services

JSB Bursar and Education Services
21 Brecklands
Mundford
Norfolk IP26 5EF
Tel: 0842 878672
Fax: 0842 878672

Montessori St Nicolas Centre
23–24 Princes Gate
Knightsbridge
London SW7 1PT
Tel: 071 225 1277
Fax: 071 823 7557

National Association of Governors and Managers
26 Laystall Street
London EC1R 4PQ
Tel: 071 833 0399

National Association of Head Teachers
1 Heath Square
Boltro Road
Haywards Heath
West Sussex RH16 1BL
Tel: 0444 458133
Fax: 0444 416326

The National Primary Centre
Westminster College
North Hinksey
Oxford OX2 9AT
Tel: 0865 245242

Roehampton Institute
School of Education
Froebel College
Roehampton Institute
Roehampton Lane
London SW15 5PJ

The School of Education
University of Birmingham
Edgbaston
Birmingham B15 2TT
Tel/Fax: 021 414 4865

School of Management and Finance
Nottingham University
University Park
Nottingham NG7 2RD
Tel: 0602 515486
Fax: 0602 515503

Secondary Heads' Association (MAPS)
130 Regent Road
Leicester LE1 7PG
Tel: 0533 471797

Sheffield Hallam University
School of Education
Collegiate Crescent Campus
Sheffield S10 2BP
Tel: 0742 532319/532306
Fax: 0742 532471

Somerset Education Services
Somerset County Council
County Hall
Taunton
Somerset TA1 4DV
Tel: 0823 333451
Fax: 0823 338139

Teacher Placement Service – UBI
Sun Alliance House
New Inn Hall Street
Oxford OX1 2QE
Tel: 0865 722585

Training consultants and career development

Barleythorpe Management Resources
Oakham
Rutland
Leicestershire
Tel: 0572 723711
Fax: 0572 757657

Careers and Occupational Information Centre (COIC)
W1108 Moorfoot
Sheffield S1 4PQ
Tel: 0742 594564

COIC (Scotland)
247 St John's Road
Edinburgh EH12 7XD
Tel: 031 334 0353

**Counselling and Career
Development Unit (CCDU)**
The University of Leeds
22 Clarendon Place
Leeds LS2 9JY
Tel: 0532 334920
Fax: 0532 334921

**Genesis Development
International**
Viking House
Swallowdale Road
Hemel Hempstead
Hertfordshire
Tel: 0442 232124
Fax: 0442 232127

**Professional Development
Consultancy**
Hucclecote Centre
Churchdown Lane
Hucclecote
Gloucester
Tel: 0452 623068
Fax: 0452 623037

Workshops

Letterbox Library
Unit 20
Lerby House
436 Essex Road
London N1 3QP
Tel: 071 226 1633
Fax: 071 226 1768

Index of Advertisers